Let the Church Sing On!
Reflections on Black Sacred Music

Let the Church Sing On!

Reflections on Black Sacred Music

James Abbington

Foreword by
Robert J. Batastini

GIA Publications, Inc.
Chicago

G-7635
Let the Church Sing On!: Reflections on Black Sacred Music
Compilation Copyright © 2009, GIA Publications, Inc.
7404 S. Mason Ave., Chicago, IL 60638

www.giamusic.com

ISBN: 978-1-57999-771-7

Book layout: Robert M. Sacha
Cover design: Martha Chlipala

Dedicated to

The Reverend Dr. Charles G. Adams, Senior Pastor,
and the choirs and congregation of
Hartford Memorial Baptist Church, Detroit, Michigan.

Contents

Foreword

Throughout his career and especially during the past decade, Dr. James Abbington has emerged as one of the principal voices in the world of African American worship and music. He has risen to that stature both as performing musician and scholar—equally at home on the organ or piano bench, at the conductor's podium, or on the dais in the lecture hall of a major university.

Whether conducting the 1,000-voice choir at the Hampton University Ministers' Conference, directing the 24-voice professional recording choir comprised of students and alumni of Morgan State University, or sitting at the console of the pipe organ at Sunday worship, he displays a masterful command of the gamut of church music, with an unrivaled expertise in the music of the African American church. Whether delivering a plenary address to the participants at a worship and music conference, or leading a music reading session or church music workshop, he has an extraordinary ability to fully engage his listeners while communicating a deep knowledge of—and passion for—the subject matter at hand.

James Abbington's scholarship is unmistakably present in his writing. In addition to his own books, he has written informative articles and essays for periodicals and journals and contributed valuable forewords, introductions, and chapters to books by other established writers. Bringing these writings together into one volume has resulted in a unique and informative compilation that is vital to pastors, musicians, students, and worshipers who cultivate an interest in both the legacy and the future development of music in the African American church.

—Robert J. Batastini
Past President and Fellow,
The Hymn Society in the United States and Canada
Retired Senior Editor, GIA Publications, Inc.

Introduction

In 1997, I was invited to be an associate editor for the *African American Heritage Hymnal* published by GIA Publications in Chicago. A sampler of that hymnal was released at the 2000 Hampton University Ministers' Conference and Choir Directors' and Organists' Guild Workshop in Hampton, Virginia. The hymnal debuted the following year at that same conference and has become the best-selling African American Protestant hymnal, having sold over 330,000 copies; it is perhaps the most significant addition to Protestant hymnody within the past century. At that time, I had no idea what a marvelous and exciting musical journey I was about to embark on with GIA Publications.

In 1999, I was asked by Ed Harris, then-President, and Robert J. Batastini, then-Senior Editor and Vice President, to become Executive Editor of the African American Church Music Series, a groundbreaking effort for the company. GIA Publications has become—and continues to be—a tremendous asset for music and worship in the Black church specifically, and the Christian church generally. Today the African American Church Music Series contains nearly 200 choral octavos by Black composers and arrangers, including anthems, hymn arrangements, spirituals, and traditional and contemporary gospel selections. In addition, I have been privileged to edit, compile, and co-author several books and worship resources, as well as conduct numerous recording projects.

Over the past few years, I have been asked by other publishers, organizations, and authors to write articles, chapters, performance columns, and introductory essays. Because many of these writings have heretofore been unknown to readers who are interested in music and worship in the Black church, I have collected them into one convenient volume. GIA Publications realized the value of such a book and eagerly accepted my proposal.

As I contemplated a title for this book, the words of an old Negro spiritual that I heard at Morehouse College as an undergraduate student immediately came to mind: "Let the Church Roll On!" One of the verses includes the phrase "Let the church sing on!" This seemed an appropriate title in an era when congregational singing, once a major component and distinctive element of Black church music and worship, is rapidly becoming extinct. The tradition of congregational singing is being replaced by praise-and-worship teams and "special" soloists or vocal ensembles; as a result, congregations have now become audiences waiting for the "entertainment." Congregational singing in the Black church has been referred to as "unity music" and a device for creating community; folk spirituals, hymns, and gospel music have helped form, develop, inspire, and liberate the Black church over the centuries and have brought us "this far by faith, leaning on the Lord"!

I have divided this compilation into three sections: (1) The Spiritual, (2) Pioneering and Contemporary Hymn Writers, and (3) Pastoral Considerations and Worship Resources. Also included are a bibliography and a discography. I am most grateful to those who granted permission to reprint the chapters in this book; they are acknowledged on pages 51–53. It is my sincere hope that these reflections will inspire, inform, and edify the reader and enhance and enlarge their knowledge of music in the Black church. Chapters 8–10 place particular emphasis on "pastoral" considerations, a term that I use not only for pastors, but for all those who shepherd, oversee, and care for God's people in music and worship.

I am indebted to many for the development of this book and I would be remiss in my responsibilities if I did not recognize a number of credit-worthy individuals. Words fail to provide adequate thanks to the staff of GIA Publications, particularly Alec Harris (President), Kelly Dobbs Mickus (Senior Editor), Michael Boschert (Permissions Editor), Garrett Jackson (Editorial and Marketing Assistant for African American Editions) and Brian Streem (Managing Editor). Thanks are also due Martha Chlipala (cover design) and Robert M. Sacha (layout).

Many thanks are extended to the community of Candler School of Theology at Emory University in Atlanta: Jan Love (Dean), Gail O'Day (Senior Associate Dean), my inspiring and supportive colleagues, and last, but not least, my students. I am grateful for friends and family who are on this journey with me, especially my mother for her unfailing love and prayers. My gratitude is endless!

My hopes for singing in the Black church—and all Christian churches that sing—cannot be expressed any better than in the following admonition from The Reverend Dr. Charles G. Adams, Senior Pastor of Hartford Memorial Baptist Church in Detroit, where I was minister of music and organist for thirteen years. These words were printed in the program of the 1992 "We Sing Praises" concert by Hartford Memorial's Jubilee Chorus:

> The aim of all church choirs is to sing with the intensity of conviction that can move the souls of people who feel jaded, empty, and defeated by the deadening oppressions, dynamics, and confusions of post-modern culture. Even the strictest of music can be made spiritually dynamic and convincing if it is sung with enthusiasm and ecstasy. On the other hand, conviction that is not informed and enthusiasm that is not controlled will not be edifying. Undisciplined enthusiasm repels rather than attracts. Uncontrolled light blinds rather than illumines.

Reverend Adams' charge most appropriately summarizes the ultimate intent for the church choir and the congregation:

> Sing on, choir!
> Sing until the emptiness of materialistic cravings are filled
>   with the transformative challenges of transcendent truth.
> Sing until dead hopes are revived, dead souls are resurrected,
>   and dead values emerge from the cold tombs of expedient
>   compromise.
> Sing until people are persuaded to love and young minds are
>   drawn to Christ.
> Sing until the preacher can preach and the church gets right.
> Sing until the power of the Lord comes down!

Let the Church Sing On!

—James Abbington
Associate Professor of Church Music and Worship
Candler School of Theology, Emory University, Atlanta, Georgia
and
Executive Editor
African American Church Music Series
GIA Publications, Inc., Chicago, Illinois

The Spiritual

elements critical for good performance of
the spiritual"
1) texts   2) tempo   3) rhythm

"Less is more" for performance of Balm in Gilead

Chapter

1

"There Is a Balm in Gilead": Metamorphosis and Implications for Performance

In her book *The Measure of Our Success: A Letter to My Children and Yours*, Marian Wright Edelman, president of the Children's Defense Fund, wrote:

> When I don't know what to do, which way to go, or feel profoundly inadequate to the task at hand, an echo of my father's frequently off-key humming of the spiritual "There Is a Balm in Gilead" wells in my heart, reminding me that I don't have to preach like the Apostle Paul or Martin King or Jesse Jackson or meet Harvard or Yale or congressional or White House or society's decreed standard of anything to be a useful messenger or servant in the world.[1]

There is probably no other spiritual more popular and beautiful as "Balm in Gilead" that expresses the predominant experience of hope and healing that has been the center of the African American experience since the beginning of slavery and has always received direct expression in the spirituals. As Marian Wright Edelman's reflections illustrate, "the lessons of the spirituals are simple yet profound and are uncluttered with the

"There Is a Balm in Gilead": Metamorphosis and Implications for Performance
Originally published in a slightly different form in *The Hymn: A Journal of Congregational Song* 58, no. 2 (2007): 44–48. Used by permission. All rights reserved.

tangential distractions and 'shoulds' that come from other voices and other places."[2]

Howard Thurman, poet, mystic, philosopher, theologian, and one of the most knowledgeable interpreters of the spirituals, has highlighted this point in his profound and prophetic exegesis of "Balm in Gilead" in his classic *Deep River and The Negro Spiritual Speaks of Life and Death:*

> The peculiar genius of the Negro slave is revealed here in much of its structural splendor. The setting is the Book of Jeremiah. The prophet has come to a "Dead Sea" place in his life. Not only is he discouraged over the external events in the life of Israel, but he is also spiritually depressed and tortured. As a wounded animal he cried out, "Is there no balm in Gilead? Is no physician there?" It is not a question of fact that he is raising—it is not directed to any particular person for an answer. It is not addressed either to God or to Israel, but rather it is a question raised by Jeremiah's entire life. He is searching his own soul. He is stripped to the literal substance of himself, and is turned back on himself for an answer. Jeremiah is saying actually, "There must be a balm in Gilead; it cannot be that there is no balm in Gilead." The relentless winnowing of his own bitter experience has laid bare his soul to the end that he is brought face to face with the very ground and core of his own faith.
>
> The slave caught the mood of this spiritual dilemma, and with it did an amazing thing. He straightened the question mark in Jeremiah's sentence into an exclamation point: "There *is* a balm in Gilead!" Here is a note of creative triumph.
>
> The melody itself is most suggestive. It hovers around the basic scale without straying far afield. Only in one place is there a sharp lifting of a tonal eyebrow—a suggestion of escape; and then the melody swings back to work out its destiny within the zones of melodic agreement.[3]

While we do not know who authored "Balm in Gilead" or when or where it was first sung, it is interesting to note that it did not appear in *A Collection of Spiritual Songs and Hymns from Various Authors by Richard*

Allen, African Minister, the first hymnal compiled expressly for the use of a Black congregation in 1801, *Slave Songs in the United States* compiled by William Allen, Charles Ware, and Lucy McKim Garrison, generally accepted as being the first collection of American Negro folks songs in 1867, or *A Collection of Revival Hymns and Plantation Melodies* published

Figure 1.1

"Balm in Gilead" in John Work's Folk Song of the American Negro, *p.43.*

in 1883 by Marshall W. Taylor which was the first hymnal designed for use by African Americans whose membership was in the predominantly White Methodist Episcopal Church. It does not appear in *The Story of The Jubilee Singers: With Their Songs* by J. B. T. Marsh published in 1880 or the subsequent 1881, 1892, or 1900 editions.

To my knowledge, the first printed version of "Balm in Gilead" appeared in *Folk Song of the American Negro* by John Wesley Work (1871–1925) originally published in 1915 by Fisk University Press in Nashville, TN, in B Major in 2/4.[4]

In 1921 it appeared in *Gospel Pearls* published by the Sunday School Publishing Board of the National Baptist Convention, USA, which was a collection of African American church music popular during the early twentieth century.[5] It later appeared in *Religious Folk-Songs of the Negro: As Sung at Hampton Institute* edited by Robert Nathaniel Dett (1882–1943) in 1927, and *Spirituals Triumphant Old and New* edited and arranged by Edward Boatner.[6] Dett's arrangement, also in B Major, found in a section labeled "Hymns of Consolation," includes a note "Transcribed from the singing of the Hampton Institute students by R. Nathaniel Dett."[7] Dett marked it "Andante molto espressivo (quarter note) = 60." It contains extensive dynamic markings and a fermata over the words "whole" and "soul".

Today the spiritual appears in most mainline denominational hymnals. Listed here are several of the most current:

African American Heritage Hymnal . . . . No. 524
AME Bicentennial Hymnal . . . . No. 425
Chalice Hymnal . . . . No. 501
Evangelical Lutheran Hymnal . . . . No. 614
Gather Comprehensive . . . . No. 648
Hymnal: A Worship Book . . . . No. 627
Lead Me, Guide Me . . . . No. 157
Lift Every Voice and Sing II . . . . No. 203
The Baptist Hymnal . . . . No. 269
The Hymnal 1982 . . . . No. 676
The New Century Hymnal. . . . . No. 553
The New National Baptist Hymnal—21st Century Edition . . . No. 489
The Presbyterian Hymnal. . . . . No. 394
The United Methodist Hymnal . . . . No. 375

Two significant sources have influenced implications for the performance of "Balm in Gilead." The first is R. Nathaniel Dett's transcription and arrangement that appears in *Religious Folk-Songs of the Negro* and William L. Dawson's (1899–1990), famous choral arrangement first published in 1939 by the Music Press of Tuskegee Institute, Tuskegee, AL, now published by Neil A. Kjos Music Publishers. These sources have informed, influenced, and shaped many of the arrangements and interpretations that are found in the aforementioned current hymnals.

Three critical elements for consideration are essential for a good performance of the spiritual. They are (1) texts, (2) tempo, and (3) rhythm. There have been several adaptations, textual revisions, re-orderings of verses, added texts, and rhythmic treatments of the verses. It is very interesting to note the textual changes and re-ordering of the verses found in the various hymnals. Typically it is the re-ordering of the second and third verses. The lyrics that appear in John Work's 1915 volume are:

(1) Sometimes I feel discouraged, and think my work's in vain.
     But then the Holy Spirit revives my soul again.

(2) Don't ever feel discouraged, for Jesus is your friend,
     And if you lack for knowledge, He'll ne'er refuse to lend.

(3) If you cannot preach like Peter, If you cannot pray like Paul,
     You can tell the love of Jesus, and say "He died for all."

All of the arrangements of "Balm in Gilead" in the aforementioned current hymnals are in F major or G major and have no tempo or dynamic markings. However, the texts and mood suggest a moderate and unfluctuating tempo. R. Nathaniel Dett's dynamic and tempo markings in Figure 1.2 are very helpful and represent a thoughtful treatment of the text. I suggest a slight ritard after each verse to prepare the congregation for the chorus.

The rhythm of the first measure of the verses in many of our current hymnals is notated as a dotted quarter followed by an eighth note. Some arrangements begin with a 2/4 measure followed by 4/4. For example, Marty Haugen's arrangement in *Gather Comprehensive* is very straightforward and adaptable for congregational singing.

Figure 1.2

Hymns of Consolation
There Is a Balm in Gilead

Transcribed from the singing of the
Hampton Institute students by
R. Nathaniel Dett

Andante molto espress ♩ = 60

(musical notation)

There is a Balm in Gil - e - ad, To

make the wound-ed whole, There is a Balm in

Gil-e - ad, To heal the sin - sick soul. There is a soul.

Solo *molto espress.*

Some - times I feel dis - cour-aged, And think my work's in

D. C.

vain, But then the Ho-ly Spir - it. Re - vives my soul a - gain.

2
Don't ever be discouraged
For Jesus is your friend,
And if you lack for knowledge,
He'll ne'er refuse to lend.

3
If you cannot preach like Peter,
If you cannot pray like Paul,
You can tell the love of Jesus,
You can say "He died for all.

"Balm in Gilead" in R. Nathaniel Dett's Religious Folk-Songs of the Negro, *p.88.*

22

Figure 1.3

There is a Balm in Gilead

Text: Jeremiah 8:22, African-American spiritual
Tune: BALM IN GILEAD, Irregular; African-American spiritual; acc. by Marty Haugen, b.1950, © 2003, GIA Publications, Inc.

"Balm in Gilead" from Gather Comprehensive *arranged by Marty Haugen, p. 617. Used by permission.*

Regardless of the arrangement, I advise being faithful to what is written in your hymnal for congregational singing. In other words, I think we have an obligation to respect the arranger's intent instead of creating a hybrid work of our own that suits our taste and preferences. Changing rhythms can be confusing and distracting in communal singing. In any case, keep the tempo steady.

I have used a cantor or soloist for the verses while the congregation and choir hummed the parts. I have also found that singing the verse in unison works well and the congregation is prepared for the chorus in harmony. These are simply suggestions for using the spiritual as congregational song.

Again, less is more in the performance of "Balm in Gilead" with its gently soothing melody and lyrics offering the final words on matters of suffering, struggle, oppression, rejection, and resistance. Finally, Arthur Jones reminds us that

> the ultimate message of hope and healing is found in the archetypally powerful music and lyrics of hundreds of other spirituals; it is the product of a creative tension between awareness of painful oppressive circumstances and the simultaneous envisioning of a hopeful future. This is not a naïve optimism, but rather a genuine inner transformation following from a process which consistently leads singers and listeners onto an emotionally and spiritually triumphant high plain. In this sense "Balm in Gilead" simply provides summary punctuation, the final confirmation of a transformation process constantly at work wherever singers of spirituals are found.[8]

"There is, there *is* a balm in Gilead to make the wounded whole and heal the sin-sick soul"!

Notes

1. Marian Wright Edelman, *The Measure of Our Success: A Letter to My Children and Yours.* (Boston: Beacon Press, 1992), 17–18.
2. Arthur C. Jones, *Wade in the Water: The Wisdom of the Spirituals.* (Maryknoll, NY: Orbis Books, 1993), 111.
3. Howard Thurman, *Deep River and The Negro Spiritual Speaks of Life and Death.* (Richmond, IN: Friends United Press, 1975), 55–56.
4. John Wesley Work, *Folk Song of the American Negro.* (New York: Negro Universities Press, 1915, reprinted in 1969 by Greenwood Press, Westport, CT), 43.
5. *Gospel Pearls.* (Nashville: Sunday School Publishing Board of the National Baptist Convention, USA, 1921), no. 158.

6. *Spirituals Triumphant Old and New.* edited and arranged by Edward Boatner. (Nashville: Sunday School Publishing Board of the National Baptist Convention, USA, 1927), no. 43.
7. R. Nathaniel Dett, ed., *Religious Folk-Songs of the Negro: As Sung at Hampton Institute.* (Hampton, VA: Hampton Institute Press, 1927), 88.
8. Arthur C. Jones, *Wade in the Water,* 127.

w/regard to performance:

Do not over-improvise churusy cross-genre accompaniments that violate the idromatic context of the congregational spiritual

In sum - do not distract from the text.

Tempo should compliment the text, harmonically and rhythmically, with solid syncopations where applicable.

A BAD TEMPO DESTROYS THE MESSAGE OF THE SPIRITUAL!

Best accompaniment is a faithful, accurate, and non-improvised rendering of the spiritual as it appears on the page to enable and enliven the congregation in singing. ~~gradually fading out~~ leaving the congregation to sing without piano or organ.

They should be performed w/integrity and understanding

Spirituals BI - Before Instrument
Spirituals AI - After instrument

genuine spirituals - sung by a group.
bent on expression of feelings and
not on sound effects

neo-spirituals - arranged or concert
spirituals e.g. Burleigh

gospelized spiritual - spiritual w/ a
gospel accompaniment

Chapter

2

Accompanying Unaccompanied Negro Spirituals: A Musical Oxymoron

If the title of this column seems contradictory or an oxymoron, as in "cruel kindness," it is, but it seems to best describe what I hope to present in this article. John Lovell, Jr. defines the Afro-American spiritual as... "an independent folk song, born of the union of African tradition and American socio-religious elements. It was affected to a limited extent by the American Christian evangelical tradition and Anglo-American hymn, but not . . . the so-called white spiritual."[1] A broad, yet somewhat precise definition of a spiritual for this writer's purpose, is a type of sacred folk song created by an anonymous individual or individuals of a particular group and adopted by that group for singing. Spirituals evolved out of their experiences, which express a range of emotions, feelings, hope, joy, faith, fear, sorrows, laments, or biblical themes and have no identifiable point of origin.

In her classic book, *The Sanctified Church*, Zora Neale Hurston clearly differentiates and distinguishes the misconception between "genuine" spirituals and what she refers to as "neo-spirituals." Referring to the "genuine" spiritual, she asserts:

Accompanying Unaccompanied Negro Spirituals: A Musical Oxymoron
Originally published in a slightly different form in *The Hymn: A Journal of Congregational Song* 58, no. 1 (2007): 47–50. Used by permission. All rights reserved.

. . . The jagged harmony is what makes it, and it ceases to be what it was when this is absent. Neither can any group be trained to produce it. Its truth dies under training like flowers under hot water. The harmony of the true spiritual is not regular. The dissonances are important and not to be ironed out by the trained musician. The various parts break in at any old time. Falsetto often takes the place of regular voices for short periods. Keys change. Moreover, each singing of the piece is a new creation. The congregation is bound by no rules. No two times singing is alike, so that we must consider the rendition of a song not a final thing, but as a mood. It will not be the same thing next Sunday. *Negro songs to be heard truly must be sung by a group, and a group bent on expression of feelings and not on sound effects.*[2]

Hurston's description of the performance practices of "genuine" spirituals, or what I call "congregational or sacred folk" spirituals, must not to be confused with what she calls "neo-spirituals," or the arranged or concert spirituals by such composer/arrangers as Harry T. Burleigh, Hall Johnson, William Dawson, Margaret Bonds, JamesWeldon and J. Rosamond Johnson, R. Nathaniel Dett, Undine Smith Moore, Jester Hairston, Roland Carter, Moses Hogan, Andre Thomas, Uzee Brown, Jr., and many others. There are many arrangements of spirituals with piano accompaniment wherein, like German folk texts and melodies that were elevated to become art song presentations, as in the Volkslieder of Johannes Brahms, the accompaniment functions very much as a dual partner in illumining texts. Dr. Uzee Brown, Jr., Professor of Music at Morehouse College says "In addition to undergirding the solo voice, the accompaniment in the solo performance of spirituals quite often fills the role of the responsorial body in what would have been indigenously presented as group or congregational singing." This is clearly illustrated in his extraordinary spiritual collections *O Redeemed* and *Trying to Make Heaven My Home* published by Roger Dean Publishing Company.[3]

John W. Work, III, addressing the 1961 International Hymnological Conference in New York City, offers this critical insight for our under-standing of Negro spirituals:

The classical spirituals, these songs whose forms evolved among the unlettered Negro folk of the nineteenth century, were conceived as linear music, without the aid of the keyboard. Other musical instruments—fiddles, guitars, etc.—were forbidden by Church policy. The song creators conceived the spirituals without the use of keyboard, and the congregation sang them without keyboard support or the experience of listening to a keyboard. These songs had no preconceived harmony, and in the rural churches they were sung without harmony. Such harmony as one might have heard was an incidental alto or a tenor supplied by individuals who might have had keyboard experience. Occasionally, one heard a bass singing the melody two octaves below the soprano, but never is a real bass part encountered. But in spite of the spiritual's incubation in a purely linear style, the melodies of the spirituals lend themselves readily to four-part harmonization.[4]

Today we have several four-part harmonizations of spirituals in denominational hymnals and other collections. These settings are the creation of the arranger to capture a fixed melody of the spiritual with accessible harmony and rhythm suitable for congregational singing representative of an oral tradition that was not notated. Work adds ". . . in folk congregational singing, harmony is rare and, where it does occur, it is only incidental. But an important purveyor and creator of spirituals, the folk quartet or folk ensemble does use harmony and a style of free counterpoint to a remarkable degree. The tonic, dominant, and subdominant chords with various added notes are their chief stock in trade."[5] In the spiritual "New Born Again" arranged by Roland Carter in the *African American Heritage Hymnal,* he successfully captures the congregational idiom and quartet-style bass line commonly heard in churches that still sing spirituals. His arrangement provides all of the musical ingredients needed for a great congregational spiritual and should only be accompanied as he wrote it.

In the same address to the 1961 International Hymnological Conference, John Work declared:

29

About thirty years ago, in the new kind of gospel song which emerged, the piano was added to the music of the folk church. Not only did the piano bring dance rhythms to the music, but it also brought a harmonic texture out of which the new melodies and a new type of melody—an inferior type of melody—grew. I choose to call the new gospel songs the *new spirituals*. They are created by the same folk who created the older spirituals. They serve the same folk worship function. But now harmony becomes an important factor in the folk church, although it is subordinate to the new dance rhythms . . . In another folk church, the Holiness Church, other instruments—the tambourine, guitar, and some woodwind instruments—have been added to the musical accompaniment.[6]

What Work is describing here is what I call the "gospelized-spiritual," a spiritual with a gospel accompaniment added to the four-part setting for congregational singing. In "We Are Climbing Jacob's Ladder" arranged by Horace Boyer, a rather challenging accompaniment has been provided which certainly does not need any improvisation. Boyer arranged this spiritual for choir and congregation and adds a newly composed section specifically for choir. However in "Guide My Feet" arranged by Avis Graves, a more accessible accompaniment is provided and can be improvised. She also adds a newly composed section not originally found in the spiritual. It is an excellent example of the "gospelized-spiritual" for choir and congregation.

I must caution pianists to be very careful not to over-improvise clumsy, cross-genre, Broadway, jazzy accompaniments that violate the idiomatic context of the congregational spiritual. John Work suggested that "any discussion of spirituals should be labeled Spirituals BI (spirituals before instruments) and Spirituals AI (spirituals after instruments)."[7] While many accompanists treat these two categories recklessly and feel that the spiritual needs to "jazzed-up heavily gospelized," it not only distracts from the texts, but creates a distasteful stylistic rendition. It has been said before and certainly applies to accompanying unaccompanied Negro spirituals—"Less is more!" It is congregational music, not solo instrumental music with congregational accompaniment. In the words of James Cone:

"Black music is unity music. It unites the joy and sorrow, the love and the hate, the hope and despair of Black people. . . It shapes and defines Black people and creates cultural structures for Black expression. Black music is unifying because it...affirms that Black being is possible only in a communal context."[8]

Another observation is that spirituals are generally taken too fast. The tempo should enhance and complement the text, harmonically and rhythmically, with solid syncopations where applicable. The mood of the spiritual is critical to tempo decisions. A bad tempo will destroy the message of the spiritual. They are not meant to be comical, light-hearted, flippant, or entertaining. For example, the spiritual "There Is a Balm in Gilead" profoundly straightens out the question marks at the end of Jeremiah 8:22—"Is there no balm in Gilead; is there no physician there? Why then is not the health of the daughter of my people recovered?"— to an affirmative exclamation point which resounds "There *is*, there *is* a balm in Gilead to heal the sin-sick soul!"

The best and most effective accompaniment of Negro spirituals is a faithful, accurate, and non-improvised rendering of the spiritual as it appears on the page to enable and enliven the congregation in singing gradually fading out leaving the congregation to sing without the piano or organ. This *a cappella* rendering is most authentic to original practices cited by Hurston and Work. Negro spirituals were originally sung without accompaniment until the generation of the "new spirituals," or gospelized-spirituals came into existence strongly influenced by the Holiness-Pentecostal movement. Some of the most common include "I Woke Up This Morning," "This Little Light of Mine," "Old Time Religion," "We Are Climbing Jacob's Ladder," "Guide My Feet While I Run this Race," and "Go Tell It on the Mountain."

While the Negro spirituals have no ownership or readily identifiable point of origin, they exist for everyone and should be performed with the same integrity and understanding of Taizé, German chorales, plainsong, shaped-note singing, or any other global sacred music.

Notes

1. John Lovell, Jr. *Black Song: The Forge and the Flame* (New York: MacMillan, 1972), 111.
2. Zora Neale Hurston. *The Sanctified Church* (Berkeley, CA: Turtle Island Press, 1981), 79–80.
3. *O Redeemed! A Set of African-American Spirituals* (30/1067) and *Tryin' to Make Heaven My Home* (30/1778R) by Uzee Brown, Jr. are both available from Roger Dean Publishing Company, A Division of the Lorenz Corporation, P. O. Box 802, Dayton, OH 45401-0802.
4. John W. Work, III. "The Negro Spiritual" in *Readings in African American Church Music and Worship* edited by James Abbington (Chicago: GIA Publications, 2001), 18–19.
5. Ibid., 19.
6. Ibid., 20.
7. Ibid., 20.
8. James Cone. *The Spiritual and the Blues* (Maryknoll, NY: Orbis Books, 1972), 5.

[handwritten notes at top of page:] Blacks adapted and adopted their own unique fashion and style to their music in response to their testimonies about the goodness of God

Chapter

3

[handwritten:] hymns are not spirituals or black-metered music,

Spirits That Dwell in Deep Woods— Editor's Preface

I am absolutely delighted to have the task of editing this marvelous collection of *Prayer and Praise Hymns of the Black Religious Experience* by The Reverend Dr. Wyatt Tee Walker. I was privileged to meet Dr. Walker at the Hampton University Ministers' and Musicians' Conference in the mid-1980s and have shared many wonderful musical experiences with him over the years. He is an unswerving model of academic excellence, head and heart, Athens and Jerusalem, reason and revelation, pastor and scholar. As former Director of Music for the Progressive National Baptist Convention, Inc. (1990–1994) and instructor for the National Congress of Christian Education, I was fortunate to have Dr. Walker as a visiting lecturer in our Black Sacred Music class and share his rich and unparalleled experience with the students from time to time. His classic, *Somebody's Calling My Name: Black Sacred Music and Social Change* was the first on the subject and laid the foundation for the work and research of such scholars as J. Wendell Mapson, Jr., Melva Wilson Costen, Jon Michael Spencer, William B. McClain, this writer, and countless others.

Spirits That Dwell in Deep Woods—Editor's Preface
Originally published in a slightly different form in *Spirits That Dwell in Deep Woods: The Prayer and Praise Hymns of the Black Religious Experience*, Wyatt Tee Walker, ed. James Abbington (Chicago: GIA Publications, Inc., 2003), ix–x. All rights reserved.

When Dr. Walker introduced *Spirits That Dwell in Deep Woods* in 1987, it was enthusiastically received and much needed at a time that seemed to have totally discarded and replaced the early music of the African American religious experience with the contemporary, popular, and commercialized music of the time. Dr. Walker's work and subsequent *Spirits That Dwell in Deep Woods II* (1988) and *Spirits That Dwell in Deep Woods III* (1991), provided the African American church with an extremely vital and important missing link to what we call African American church music today, specifically, gospel music. However, this collection was not nearly as widely known and used as a resource for worship and research. I have personally introduced many of these sacred gems in workshops, worship, lectures, and concerts that I have conducted throughout this country, but have been disappointed that this collection is not listed in African American sacred music bibliographies or available in most African American religious bookstores.

Last year, Dr. Walker and I were seated together on a flight from Norfolk, VA, having left the Hampton University Ministers' and Musicians' Conference early to attend the funeral of the late Reverend Dr. Nathaniel Tyler-Lloyd, former pastor of the Trinity Baptist Church in Bronx, NY, a dear mutual friend. During our conversation, he shared his respect, praises, and appreciation for the work that GIA Publications was contributing to the publishing of music for the African American church in general, and for the recently released *African American Heritage Hymnal* specifically, for which he served on the Editorial Committee. It was at that point that I seized the opportunity to ask him for permission to edit and republish *Spirits That Dwell in Deep Woods* into one volume, to which he immediately responded by reaching for the pen in his suit pocket saying, "Where do I sign?" GIA's interest was immediate and enthusiastic, and one year later, that dream has become a reality.

In this awe-inspiring collection, all twenty-four of the *Prayer and Praise Hymns* in the previously published volumes appear in alphabetical order with the text, an introduction, biblical basis, theological mooring, lyric and form analysis, and contemporary significance provided by Dr. Walker. The forwards to Volume I and II written by The Reverend Dr. Gardner C. Taylor, Pastor Emeritus of the Concord Baptist Church of Christ in Brooklyn, NY, and Volume III written by The Reverend Dr. Jeremiah A. Wright, Jr., Senior Pastor of the Trinity United Church of Christ in Chicago, IL, appear in the pages before Dr. Walker's prefaces to all three volumes. The acknowledgments for all three volumes are found at the end of the *Prayer and Praise Hymns*.

In Dr. Walker's Introduction he explains:

> The *Prayer and Praise Hymns* have been an integral part of the sacred hymnody of the Black religious experience. Following the disappointment of the Post-reconstruction era, Black religious practice turned increasingly inward. Though the children of slaves borrowed from and adapted some of the worship styles of the dominant society (whites), the practical reality of the separateness in American life induced in African Americans, a form of self-reliance so far as the character of our worship styles were concerned. Black people trudged ahead with their Africanized version of Christianity, coping as best we could with the persistent presence of racism and color prejudice.
>
> Emigration from the rural South was not widespread. At the turn of the century, large numbers of Black Americans remained in the countryside working the land they owned or sharecropping. It was in the rural South, principally, that these hymns were born.
>
> These hymns are not *spirituals* in either the technical or historical sense. All authentic *spirituals* antedated the end of the Civil War. Neither are they *black meter music* in any sense, though much of the verbiage is drawn from the bright imagery of the latter part of the meter music era. They are adaptations of what rural Blacks heard around them religiously. The poetry and musicality of the *Prayer and Praise Songs* are distinct from that of spirituals and Black meter music.
>
> In time frame, these songs are spin-offs of the early hymn-book era in Black religious life (c. 1885–1925). They are in every sense, folk-music of the Black religious experience. Like the spirituals, in this respect, there are no identifiable authors. The body of this music expresses in individual form the collective consciousness of the

community in matters of religious belief. There is in this music the flavor of both *Spiritual and Black Meter Music* without any real loss of its own identity.

As seventeenth-century enslaved Africans heard sermons and testimonies of God's goodness, love, grace, mercy, and deliverance, they created songs in response to them. Those they did not create, they adapted and adopted in their own unique style, fashion, and liking. While the four-part musical settings provided by C. Eugene Cooper, provide the most accurate rendering of these *Prayer and Praise Hymns*, one must be sensitive and knowledgeable of the performance practices of the early African American church that "blackened" them, once stated by the late Wendell P. Whalum. Where the rhythm was straight, they syncopated it. Where they found the meter consistent, they made it inconsistent. If the tempo was too fast, they slowed it down. If the tempo was too slow, they took it faster. If the melody was too simple, they ornamented and embellished it. In her book, *The Sanctified Church*, Zora Neale Hurston asserts, "...The jagged harmony is what makes it, and it cease to be what it is when it is absent. Neither can any group be trained to produce it...the various parts break in at any old time. Falsetto often takes the place of regular voices for short periods." In essence, they made the songs their own.

I owe a tremendous debt of gratitude to my GIA family, especially Alec Harris, President, Robert Batastini, Senior Editor and Vice President, Robert Sacha, graphic designer and Vicki Krystanski, editorial assistant. Without them, this would not have been possible.

Listed below are the selections found in this compilation:

1. Another Day's Journey and I'm So Glad
2. Blessed Be the Name of the Lord
3. Daniel in the Lion's Den
4. Glory, Glory! Hallelujah
5. Great Change Since I've Been Born
6. I Know His Blood Has Made Me Whole
7. I Know I Got Religion, Yes, Yes!
8. I Know My Name Is Written There
9. I Wanna' Be Ready

10. I Wanna' Die Easy
11. I'm Glad I Got That Old Time Religion
12. Jesus Is a Rock in a Weary Land
13. Jesus on the Main Line
14. Keep Your Lamps Trimmed and Burning
15. Lord Have Mercy
16. Nobody But You Lord
17. Satan, We're Gonna' Tear Your Kingdom Down
18. Something Happened When He Saved Me
19. Something on the Inside Working on the Outside
20. Talkin' 'Bout a Good Time
21. Till I Die, Till I Die
22. You Better Min'
23. You Better Run
24. You Can't Make Me Doubt Him

It is my sincere hope and anticipation that this magnificent music will find its way back into the repertoire of the African American church, not just in February for Black History Month or on special occasions that memorialize and commemorate the past, but that celebrates a living Christ and hope for the living of *these* days.

Pioneering and Contemporary Hymn Writers

Chapter

4

Bishop Charles Price Jones (1865–1949)

"When I first gave myself to the Lord to be sanctified (this was in 1894 at Selma), I had no idea at all of taking up holiness as a fad, or an -ism, or a creed, or a slogan of a 'cult.' I just wanted to be personally holy. I just wished to make my own calling and election sure to my own heart by walking with God in the Spirit. As a Baptist I had doctrinal assurance; I wanted spiritual assurance, heart peace, rest of soul, the joy of salvation in the understanding of a new heart, a new mind, a new spirit, constantly renewed by and comforted by the Holy Ghost.

"One day as I staggered under the weight of this obligation, under the necessity of this ministry, I felt that I must be alone and especially talk with God about it…The Spirit spoke within from the holy of holies of my redeemed spirit, and said, 'You shall write the hymns for your people.' This He said six or seven times till it was fixed in my mind. I got up and went to the organ in the corner of the room, wrote a song titled 'Praise the Lord,' ruled off a tablet, set it to music, and sang it before I left the room."

—Charles Price Jones[1]

Bishop Charles Price Jones (1865–1949)
Originally published in a slightly different form in *The African American Pulpit* 9, no. 1:23–25. Used by permission. All rights reserved.

Bishop Charles P. Jones was born December 9, 1865 in Kingston, Georgia (between Rome and Atlanta). He was converted at age 19 and accepted the call to preach at age 20. He graduated from Arkansas Baptist College in 1891. His acclaimed preaching ministry carried him from Arkansas to Alabama, and then to Jackson, Mississippi. In 1894 he was pastor of the Tabernacle Baptist Church in Selma, Alabama. He became pastor of the Mount Helm Baptist Church of Jackson, Mississippi, in 1895.

In 1896 Bishop Jones helped found what became the Church of Christ (Holiness) U.S.A. David Daniels, church historian and ordained minister in the Church of God in Christ, argues:

> [T]he Holiness movement in Mississippi, under the leadership of Charles Price Jones and Charles Harrison Mason, was able to reject the negative attitude toward slave religion that the [so-called] progressives held and yet advocate the moral, ecclesial, liturgical, and pastoral reforms that the progressives embraced. One of Jones's principal contributions to the movement was linking salvation to the formation of character, which he envisioned as a more important foundation of society than family, politics, economics, or even the church.[2]

In searching music history, one finds the name of Charles Price Jones missing from tables of contents and indexes. Yet his musical contributions were unique, voluminous, and worthy of significant mention in the legacy of American hymnody and church music literature. He wrote more than one thousand gospel songs, most of them between 1895–1905. While his creativity and ingenuity are familiar to the Church of Christ (Holiness) U.S.A, people over much of the United States and many parts of the world have been inspired by the songs of C. P. Jones.

According to Anita B. Jefferson, a Church of Christ (Holiness) U.S.A. member who was involved in a 2000 reprint of Jones's *An Appeal to the Sons of Africa,* "C. P. Jones's songs were born out of a deep love for God and a life totally committed to God. Jones's song sprang from a soul fed from a well supplied by fasting and feasting on God's word along with communing deeply with Him. His life was not a shallow one of selfishness, worldliness, and pleasure."[3]

The "Ministry of Song," as Bishop Jones referred to his song writing, was one of the most prominent stimuli during the denominational emergence of the Church of Christ (Holiness) U.S.A. Rev. Jones's vast and rich corpus of original hymnody (comprised of hymns and anthems, almost all of which he personally set to music) is an amazing accomplishment unmatched by any African American songwriter of religious music before or since.

Two years following the inaugural Holiness Convention of 1897 (the official founding date of the denomination), Jones's first songbook, *Jesus Only* (1899), appeared. The promotional copy on the back cover read, "Jesus Only, No. 1—For all religious services; songs of the higher Christ life… They express your soul's deepest devotion in catchy, yet most appropriate tunes."[4] *Jesus Only* proved to be only the first of a prolific production of songbooks. Jones published *Jesus Only,* Nos. 1 and 2 in 1901.

In ensuing years, *Select Songs* appeared, containing the African hymn of hope, "Stretch Your Hand to God," and "Wanted—Men." *Select Songs* was said to contain songs for emancipation celebrations and other occasions. Still later came *His Fulness* (1906), then *Sweet Selections*, both of which Jones described as "jewels…precious in the spiritual life of the church."[5] The official hymnal of the Church of Christ (Holiness) U.S.A. is Jones's *His Fulness Songs,* republished by the National Publishing Board of the Church of Christ (Holiness) U.S.A. in 1977. It features one of the most important songs written by Bishop Jones, "Jesus Only," the opening hymn in both volumes of *Jesus Only;* it also contains one of my personal favorites, "I Will Make the Darkness Light."

Not only did Jones write songs, he was known for his desire to lift up his race and his love of Africa. His book *An Appeal to the Sons of Africa: A Number of Poems, Readings, Orations and Lectures Designed Especially to Inspire Youth of African Blood* is an amazing compilation of materials that show Jones as an unusual sage of his time. Included are pieces such as "Don't Tom," "Honor the Old Man," "Treat the Young Man Well," and "Liberia." Space does not permit the listing of all of Bishop Jones's publications.

Because we must keep alive Jones's rich hymnody, which is a significant part of black religious and cultural heritage, and because this music is central to discussions of American hymnody, "I Will Make the

Darkness Light" and "Jesus Only" are printed on the following pages (see Figures 4.1 and 4.2, respectively) with the permission of the presiding bishop of the denomination, Bishop Emery Lindsay.

Notes

1. Charles Price Jones, "Autobiographical Sketch of Charles Price Jones," in Otho B. Cobbins, ed., *History of Church of Christ (Holiness) U.S.A.*, 1895–1965 (New York: Vantage Press, 1966), 23–25.
2. David Douglass Daniels II, "The Cultural Renewal of Slave Religion: Charles Price Jones and the Emergence of the Holiness Movement in Mississippi" (Ph.D. dissertation, Union Theological Seminary, 1992), 234.
3. See *Jesus Only*, Nos. 1 and 2, back cover.
4. Ibid.
5. Charles Price Jones, "History of My Songs," in Cobbins, 422.

Figure 4.1

I WILL MAKE THE DARKNESS LIGHT

Psalms 18:28, 35:1, 27:3, 77:20, 136:16, 146:7, 107:7, 5:8, 91:2–4*

*Also see Isaiah 42:16

Figure 4.2

Jesus Only

Text: Charles P. Jones, 1865–1949
Tune: JESUS ONLY, 8 7 8 7 with refrain; Charles P. Jones, 1865–1949

Chapter

5

Beams of Heaven: Hymns of Charles Albert Tindley (1851–1933)— Introduction

Charles Albert Tindley, pastor, orator, poet, writer, theologian, social activist, "father of African American Hymnody," "progenitor of African American gospel music" and "prince of preachers," made an indelible imprint along Methodism's historic trail and was a most influential and dynamic cleric in American religion and social history. He is one of Methodism's eminent preachers, but unfortunately, very little has been written about him. Without a doubt, he ranks as one of the most effective preachers ever produced by Methodism in general and Black Methodism in particular. Carter G. Woodson said that Tindley and C. T. Walker were the two greatest preachers of power developed during the second generation of freedom.[1]

Born July 7, 1851 in Berlin, Worchester County, Maryland, Charles and Esther Tindley named their newborn son, Charles Albert. His mother

Beams of Heaven: Hymns of Charles Albert Tindley (1851–1933)—Introduction
Originally published in *Beams of Heaven: Hymns of Charles Albert Tindley (1851–1933)*, ed. S. T. Kimbrough, Jr., music ed. Carlton R. Young (New York: GBGMusik, 2006), v–xii. Used by permission. All rights reserved.

died when he was a little more than two years old and he was raised by his loving father. The assertion frequently found in biographical sketches that he was born "of slave parents," seems drawn from his reference to his "slave ancestors." However, Tindley's autobiographical statement in his *Book of Sermons* (1932) implies that he was not a slave. He recalls that because of economic hardship after his mother, Esther Miller Tindley, died, his father was forced to hire him out. "This practice was not unusual for freed Blacks. Hired-out workers often labored alongside slaves, experiencing much of the reality of the slave plantation. The major differences were that there was some remuneration (in Tindley's case, to his father) and hired-out workers did get the opportunity to go home."[2]

In Tindley's *Book of Sermons*, he describes his struggle to learn to read and comments on how this experience affected him:

> . . . It therefore became my lot to be "hired out," wherever father could place me. The people with whom I lived were not all good. Some of them were very cruel to me. I was not permitted to have a book or go to church. I used to find bits of newspaper on the roadside and put them in my bosom (for I had no pockets), in order to study the ABC's from them. During the day, I would gather pine knots, and when the people were asleep at night I would light these pine knots, and, lying flat on my stomach to prevent being seen by any one who might still be about, would, with fire-coals, mark all the words I could make out on these bits of newspaper. I continued in this way, and without any teacher, until I could read the Bible almost without stopping to spell the words.

More than eighteen years of this passed before he learned to read and write. Through personal diligence, Tindley garnered enough "information" to take the examination for the ministry.

Tindley moved to Philadelphia in his youth. For three years, he worked as a hod carrier in Philadelphia, and attended school at night. He said, "I made a rule to learn at least one new thing—a thing I did not know the day before—each day." This rule was faithfully pursued throughout his life. As a self-taught person, Tindley did not graduate from a recognized college or seminary, although he was an avid reader and accumulated more than

8,000 volumes in his library. The best information on this comes from Tindley's own words.

> Many people have asked me about my education and how I secured it. I wish I could tell all the ways and means employed for this purpose, for the sake of encouraging some boy and girl who may be as poor and unfortunate as I was. My first plan was to buy every book I could which I thought contained anything that I should know. Then I entered by correspondence, all the schools which my limited means would afford, and sought to keep up the studies with any pupil who studied in the school room. I was able to attend the Brandywine Institute and to finish its Theological course. By correspondence, I took the Greek course through the Boston Theological School and the Hebrew under Professor Speaker through the Hebrew Synagogue on North Broad Street, in Philadelphia, PA, I took my studies in Science and Literature as a private student because I was unable to attend the universities where these subjects were taught. Thus, while I was unable to go through the schools, I was able to let the schools go through me.
>
> I have picked my way up the hillside of learning and kept the fires of education burning, and by the gleams of scholarly light, I worked all day and studied all night. I measure not my task by ages, nor pick out others to be my gauge, my life has only just begun, my goal is in the sun.
>
> Bennett College (Greensboro, NC) and Morgan College, Baltimore, MD, gave me the degree of Doctor of Divinity some years ago. Before that, God had given me a real call to the ministry and the gift of the Holy Ghost.[3]

This yearning for learning buoyed Tindley to excellence. Henry H. Mitchell says ". . . Because his training did not occur in formal settings, he endured ridicule from some of his pastor peers. But his sound, powerful, colorful preaching won him many supporters."[4]

Between 1880 and 1885 Tindley was a member of the Bainbridge Street Methodist Church of Philadelphia, where he served as janitor. This congregation granted him license to preach and enabled him to become a member of the Delaware Annual Conference. In 1902 Tindley, refused reappointment as Presiding Elder (those now holding this position are termed District Superintendent) of the Salisbury District and asked for assignment to Bainbridge Street Methodist Episcopal Church. His request was reluctantly granted by the bishop for Tindley had brought a new dimension to Presiding Eldership by having rendered statistical reports and personal evaluations of ministers he supervised.

> Tindley's arrival at Bainbridge Street was not universally accepted by the congregation for several prominent officials and laypersons remembered him as the tall, gangling man from Berlin, Maryland who over ten years before had taught himself how to read and write while being the unpaid sexton of their place of worship. Others pointed out that he had never attended any school, college, or seminary, as had their previous ministers.[5]

Bainbridge Street Methodist Episcopal Church was over-crowded when Tindley appeared as pastor. Most were curious to see how he conducted himself, to hear the message he might bring, and to see whether he was still the tall, ungainly person they had known. "All were pleasantly surprised, for as Tindley mounted the rostrum, wearing a Prince Albert Coat—then the garb of many African American Protestant preachers—he had the dignified bearing acquired during his previous appointments. They were further surprised when Tindley delivered a masterful, soul gripping sermon that brought loud amens and praise God exclamations from his listeners."[6] From that moment Tindley's reputation as an outstanding preacher grew by leaps and bounds and spread throughout the country.

During the Depression, as was true of the nation, money problems plagued the congregation. The church rallied and developed a Soup Kitchen to feed and clothe the hungry and homeless. It is still in existence and has received Philadelphia's "Best Practices Award" several times.

As Tindley's reputation as a preacher continued to grow, so did the congregation. In 1924, the neighboring property was purchased and construction began on what Tindley referred to as "God's Cathedral." Tindley explained to the congregation that the new church would generally conform to the description of the twelve-gated city described in the Book of Revelation. It was a mega church before the term was coined. At the height of his ministry, the membership increased to an unheard of 12,000! In 1924, the name of the church was changed once again, this time to Tindley Temple, in honor of the distinguished pastor. A court decree accomplished this on April 25, 1927.

At age 82, Reverend Tindley's poor health weakened his 6'4" frame. After a two-week confinement in Frederick Douglass Hospital, he died on July 26, 1933.

One of Tindley's outstanding talents was his ability to write gospel hymns, which he often interpolated into his sermons. By 1912, he had composed the music and written the texts for over twenty hymns. "These were printed and sold as this became popular music for the 'saved' and 'unsaved' folk who heard them."[7] Tindley's music influenced early gospel music composers such as Thomas A. Dorsey, Lucie E. Campbell, Roberta Martin, William Herbert Brewster, and Kenneth Morris.

Horace C. Boyer offers this helpful insight:

> During his lifetime, Tindley was renowned as a gospel preacher, although today he is remembered primarily as a gospel songwriter. He was helped in his musical ministry by his eight children, all of whom exhibited a fondness and talent for musical performance, though none became composers. Emmaline, called Emma, was the most talented, a fine contralto and a skilled pianist; on more than one occasion she served as accompanist to her contemporary, contralto Marian Anderson. Charles, Jr., and Elbert served as arrangers for published versions of his music.
>
> It was not unusual for Tindley to punctuate his sermons by singing verses or choruses of his own songs. The second or third time, the congregation would join in the singing, with Tindley as leader. Beginning in the 1950s, this kind of performance would be called a gospel songfest. His sermons as well as his songs testify to a strong person, both in conviction and in musical talent. He even had the physical image of a man of strength; he has been described as a "veritable giant, six-feet-two, and weighing 230 pounds, rugged, honest, humble, compassionate."[8]

51

While Thomas A. Dorsey has been called the "father of gospel music," and rightly so, the seed that Dorsey nurtured and brought to maturity had been planted as early as the turn of the twentieth century by Tindley. The new music of the Black composers that increasingly found acceptance in the Black church was a hymn-like composition differing little from that written by such white composers as William B. Bradbury, Robert Lowry, and William Howard Doane–that is, a song with (1) its text based on conversion, salvation, and heaven; (2) its form being a two-part structure of verse and chorus, each eight bars in length; (3) its rhythm characterized by a predominance of quarter and dotted-eighth notes; and (4) its chorus performed in the antiphonal style.[9]

Boyer articulately distinguishes how Tindley moved away from this formula in several respects:

> In the first place, he concentrated on texts that gave attention to such important concerns of Black Christians as worldly sorrows, blessings, and woes, as well as the joys of the afterlife. . . . He also allowed space for his inevitable improvisation of text, melody, harmony, and rhythm, so characteristic of Black American folk and popular music. Tindley, himself a cosmopolitan person, wrote songs expressly for his congregation and other Black Christians and attempted to speak directly to them. As time has proved, he spoke not only to them but to others who found this new kind of musical structure.[10]

In 1901, Tindley published eight songs: "A Better Home," "A Stranger Cut the Rope," "After a While," "From Youth to Old Age" arranged by J. Candler Wright, "Go Wash in the Beautiful Stream," "I'll Overcome Some Day," "What Are They Doing in Heaven?" and "The Lord Will Make the Way." These songs met with unexpected success and enthusiasm. "I'll Overcome Some Day" was popular shortly after its publication, then went into a decline for a number of years. In the *Companion to the United Methodist Hymnal*, Carlton R. Young offers significant insight as to possible sources of the anthem of the USA civil rights movement of the 1960s and 1970s, "We Shall Overcome."

The first and most widely held view is that it is adapted from the optimistic refrain of Charles Albert Tindley's hymn composed in 1901,

"I'll overcome some day," titled "Ye shall overcome if ye faint not," number 18 in *New Songs of Zion*, 1941. A unique quality of this hymn is the summary refrain that follows each stanza; for example:

1. This world is one great battlefield,
     With forces all arrayed;
   If in my heart I do not yield
       I'll overcome some day.

   Refrain:
   I'll overcome some day,
   I'll overcome some day;
   If in my heart I do not yield
   I'll overcome some day. [11]

While space does not permit here, Young's extensive analysis of other sources and influences on "We Shall Overcome" in his *Companion*, such as Wesley Milgate's claim that a source of the tune of the spiritual comes from "The Sicilian Mariner's Hymn to the Virgin," is worthy of thorough investigation.

Undoubtedly, the success of Tindley's songs influenced his decision to join three other ministers, all bishops (Bishop J. S. Caldwell, Bishop L. J. Coppin, and Bishop G. L. Blackwell), to form the Soul Echoes Publishing Company at 420 South Eleventh Street in Philadelphia. The company's first publication in 1905 consisted essentially of a collection of Tindley's songs, but, in the fashion of the day, it also included well-known compositions of other composers such as Reverend B. T. Tanner's "Our Fathers' Church," Bishop L. P. Coppin's "Marching Must Be Done," Bishop Daniel A. Payne's "Hymn for Baptism," Bishop J. S. Caldwell's "Away in the Kingdom" (text only), Henry F. Lyte and William Henry Monk's "Abide With Me," Charles Wesley's "Depth of Mercy!" (set to the tune SEYMOUR), S. C. Muncie's "Promised Land," and R. William Fickland and Bishop Coppin's "My Soul Delights to Sing."

In 1909 *Soul Echoes: A Collection of Songs for Religious Meetings No. 2*, an enlarged version, was published. The preface of the collection read:

A long felt desire for songs with words of Hope, Cheer, Love, and Pity; for melodies that can sink to the depths of sorrow, and rise to the heights of joy has had most to do with the publication of this book.

It is the prayer of the publishers that these messages in rhyme shall float from soul to soul until the hills and valleys shall awake into joyful singing.

By 1916, Tindley, his two sons: Charles, Jr. and Elbert, and three other associates: J. Candler Wright, Francis A. Clark, and William D. Smith, formed Paradise Publishing Company, with which Tindley remained associated until his death. The major function of this company was to publish Tindley's songs. *New Songs of Paradise! No. 1* contained all of Tindley's compositions and a few standard hymns such as "Abide with Me," "Still, Still with Thee," and Charles Wesley's "Depth of Mercy Can There Be." The first four editions of *New Songs of Paradise* (the exclamation point was dropped from the title after No. 1) were published during Tindley's lifetime. *New Songs of Paradise, No. 6* is very significant in that it includes the entire catalogue of Tindley's songs, as well as a few questionable entries.

Tindley's most famous sermon was "Heaven's Christmas Tree." It was demanded year after year. The text of the sermon was Revelation 22:2, "In the midst of the street of it, and on either side of the river was the tree of life" (KJV). It became so popular that the church had to rent the Olympia Boxing Hall, a 5,000-capacity arena, for him to deliver his famous sermon. Olympia Arena proved too small to accommodate the many worshipers and curious nonbelievers. After the sermon, Tindley invited all who were unchurched to come to the altar for prayer. More than a hundred responded, and slightly over fifty applied for membership.[12] The second time Tindley delivered his "Heaven's Christmas Tree" sermon in the Olympia Arena all seats were occupied, but not as many people were turned away as formerly. Tindley expressed himself as disappointed when worship was completed. He was asked why. "I need a proper hymn for that sermon," he replied. "Next year I'll have one."[13] And he did![14]

This collection of Tindley's hymns and poems is a much-deserved and grossly-past-due addition to many denominational hymnals, both Catholic and Protestant. The current *United Methodist Hymnal* (1989) includes five

Tindley hymns: "Nothing Between," "Stand By Me," "Leave It There," "Beams of Heaven as I Go," and "We'll Understand It Better By and By" generally found in most denominational hymnals. *Songs of Zion (Supplement,* 1981) contains the aforementioned hymns and seven additional hymns: "I'll Overcome Some Day," "I Believe It," "Let Jesus Fix It for You," "My Secret Joy," "The Storm Is Passing Over," "I Have Found at Last the Savior," and "What Are They Doing in Heaven?" In 2001 GIA Publications published the *African American Heritage Hymnal,* an African American Protestant hymnal that included Tindley's "Heaven's Christmas Tree," "In Me," and a gospelized version of "The Storm Is Passing Over."

I conclude with an insight offered by cultural folklorist and songwriter Dr. Bernice Johnson Reagon:

> Reverend Charles Albert Tindley wrote . . . songs, whose themes cover much of the general Christian experience. When African Americans dip into the well of his music, we pull out those pieces that speak most strongly to our experience: change and struggle as keys to service and deliverance. Tindley's songs became an extension of the message he felt charged to give. As the Philadelphia congregants packed his services to absorb his sermons, so the larger African American community absorbed his songs. Like water in a dry land, these new songs gave musical energy to the twentieth-century African American sacred experience.[15]

I echo Dr. Reagon's sentiments and add that Tindley's songs have been absorbed and sung, and continue to be absorbed and sung, by non-African Americans both Catholic and Protestant. Like Martin Luther, he was a theologian, preacher, and composer whose message was as clear in his songs and poetry as they were in his sermons. These songs continue to inspire, uplift, encourage, provide hope, joy, peace, and comfort for *all* Christians in the twenty-first century and, I am certain, for generations yet unborn!

—James Abbington, D.M.A.
Associate Professor of Music and Worship
Candler School of Theology
Emory University, Atlanta, GA

Notes

1. Carter G. Woodson, *The History of the Negro Church* (Washington, DC: Associated Publishers, 1945, 1972), 222.
2. Bernice Johnson Reagon, ed., *We'll Understand It Better By and By: Pioneering African American Gospel Composers* (Washington, DC: Smithsonian Institute Press, 1992), 41.
3. Ralph Jones, *Charles Albert Tindley: Prince of Preachers* (Nashville: Abingdon, 1982), 37.
4. Henry H. Mitchell, "The Genius Composer-Preacher: Charles Albert Tindley in *The African American Pulpit* Summer 2001, 12.
5. Tindley Temple United Methodist Church (1837–1987), *150th Anniversary Journal: "Celebrating Our Heritage and Building the Future"* (Philadelphia, 1987), 3.
6. Ibid., 3.
7. Ibid., 3.
8. "Charles Albert Tindley: Progenitor of African American Gospel Music" by Horace Clarence Boyer in *We'll Understand It Better By and By: Pioneering African American Gospel Composers* edited by Bernice Johnson Reagon (Washington, DC: Smithsonian Institute Press, 1992), 55–56.
9. Ibid., 57.
10. Ibid.
11. Carlton R. Young, *Companion to The United Methodist Hymnal* (Nashville: Abingdon, 1993). 679. See the entire entry on "We Shall Overcome" on pages 679–680.
12. Ralph Jones, *Charles Albert Tindley: Prince of Preachers*, 71.
13. Ibid., 73.
14. For the complete sermon see the "Great Revivalists I" Winter 2001–2002 of *The African American Pulpit*, 50–55, or Ralph Jones's *Charles Albert Tindley: Prince of Preachers*, 145–156.
15. Bernice Johnson Reagon, *We'll Understand It Better By and By*, 52.

[Editor's Note: Information for the companion CD to *Beams of Heaven* is provided below. See the Discography for a complete list of recordings available through GIA Publications, Inc.]

Beams of Heaven

Companion CD for *Beams of Heaven: Hymns of Charles Albert Tindley (1851–1933)*, ed. S. T. Kimbrough, Jr., music ed. Carlton R. Young

Catalog No.: CD 1-025 [available through Cokesbury]

Charles Albert Tindley was a clergyman of the Methodist Episcopal Church and a founding figure in American gospel music. Born in Berlin, Maryland, in 1851, he died as pastor of a 12,500-member congregation in Philadelphia. He also wrote the words and music to dozens of gospel hymns, including five published in the current United Methodist Hymnal and others found in the Songs of Zion songbook.

Contents of CD

1. Courage, my soul
2. Thou, O Christ, my Lord and King
3. Beams of heaven
4. Tindley Organ Medley: I am a poor pilgrim of sorrow/I'm on my way/We are often tossed and driven/Beams of heaven/Reprise: The Pilgrim's Song
5. Nothing between
6. If the world from you withhold
7. A better day is coming
8. I am thinking of friends
9. Heaven's Christmas Tree
10. This world is one great battlefield
11. There was Naaman the leper
12. Ye pilgrims through this vale of tears
13. Beams of heaven
14. I have heard of a tree
15. Come, saints and sinners
16. When the storms of life are raging
17. We are often tossed and driven

Chapter

6

Suggested Interpretations for Three Gospel Hymns by Margaret Pleasant Douroux

Dr. Margaret Pleasant Douroux (b. 1941), a noted California-based minister of music, pianist, composer, music publisher, educator, author, clinician, and lecturer is considered by many to be the "Reigning Queen of African American Gospel Hymnody."

She holds degreesfrom California State College, The University of Southern California, and The University of Beverly Hills. Following in the rich legacy of African American women hymnwriters Roberta Martin, Lucie E. Campbell, and Doris Akers, Margaret Douroux's hymns are finding their way into mainline denominational hymnals and supplements. "Give Me a Clean Heart," published in 1970 and based on Psalm 51:10, first appeared in *The New National Baptist Hymnal* in 1979, (#349) arranged by Albert Denis Tessier. Later it appeared in *Lead Me, Guide Me: The African American Catholic Hymnal* in 1987 (#279), *Lift Every Voice and Sing II: An African American Hymnal* in 1993 (#124), *For the Living of These Days: Resources for Enriching Worship* (#28), *The New Century Hymnal* in 1995 (#188), *This Far by Faith: An African American Resource for Worship* in 1999 (#216), *The Faith We Sing,* compiled primarily as a supplement to

Suggested Interpretations for Three Gospel Hymns by Margaret Pleasant Douroux
Originally published in a slightly different form in *The Hymn: A Journal of Congregational Song* 58, no. 3 (2007): 48–51. Used by permission. All rights reserved.

the 1989 *United Methodist Hymnal* (#2133), and *Sing! A New Creation,* co-published by The Calvin Institute of Christian Worship, Faith Alive Christian Resources, and the Office of Worship of the Reformed Church of America, in 2002 (#64). In some instances only the chorus appears.

In 2001, "Give Me a Clean Heart" appeared in *The African American Heritage Hymnal* (#461) along with her other hymns "Day and Night Praise" (#115), "High Praise" (#181), "How Do You Recognize a Child of God" (#266), "What Shall I Render" (#389), and "One More Day" (#538). In the same year, in addition to several of the aforementioned, "Give Me a Clean Heart" appeared in *The New National Baptist Hymnal: 21*[st]*Century Edition* (#545) along with a Christmas hymn "The Angels Sang" (#99), "The Lord Is Speaking" (#169), and "Stand Still" (#519). Another very popular gospel hymn by Douroux, "If It Had Not Been for the Lord," based on Psalm 124:1 and published in 1980, first appeared in *For the Living of These Days* (#13) and *The Faith We Sing* (#2053).

Three previously unpublished gospel hymns in mainline denominational hymnals or supplements by Douroux appear in *New Wine in Old Wineskins: A Contemporary Song Supplement* (GIA) edited by this writer. They are "Count It All Joy" (#12), "Follow Jesus" (#14), and "No Trouble at the River" (#43). While these selections are well known and popular among many African American gospel musicians, singers, choirs, and congregations, they are unknown to other Christian churches in the United States. I will attempt to share suggested interpretations (from personal encounters and conversations with Douroux) and what are generally acceptable performance practices of this genre.

Count It All Joy

"Count It All Joy," inspired by James 1:2 ("My brethren, count it all joy when you fall into divers temptations"), provides the mood, attitude, and character for this hymn. A theologian once said that Christianity teaches [us] to be joyful under troubles: such exercises are sent from God's love; and trials in the way of duty will brighten our graces now, and our crown at last. In other words, instead of murmuring and complaining over trials and temptations, rejoice in them. The suggested tempo marking (the quarter note = ca. 50, or think of the eighth note = ca. 100), should remain stately, fixed, even, and constant to better articulate and enable the texts.

60

Figure 6.1

Count It All Joy

Text: Margaret Pleasant Douroux, b.1941
Tune: Margaret Pleasant Douroux, b.1941
© Rev. Earl Pleasant Publishing Co.

Excerpt from
New Wine in Old Wineskins
A Contemporary Congregational Song Supplement
GIA Publications, Inc. G-7113
Used by permission.

For an introduction, I suggest playing the hymn through once as it is written to establish tempo and the spirit in which it should be sung. There are cue notes that provide rhythmic and arpeggiated elaborations throughout. I suggest playing the bass voice in octaves, on the beat, in the left hand and the tenor as a triad in the right hand with the treble voices.

(See Figure 6.1) Occasionally playing the bass voice two octaves lower on beats one and three adds an orchestral-like quality that substitutes for an implied bass guitar. Occasional rolled-chords an octave higher in the treble voices also adds to this quasi-orchestral or full effect. However, in the first and second measures of the last system, the cues notes should be played two octaves lower with steady rhythmic energy.

Figure 6.2

Follow Jesus

Text: Margaret Pleasant Douroux, b.1941, © 1981, Rev. Earl Pleasant Publishing Co.
Tune: Margaret Pleasant Douroux, b.1941, © 1981; arr. by Kenneth W. Louis, b.1956, © 2006, GIA Publications, Inc.
Used by permission.

Follow Jesus

"Follow Jesus," listed in the topical index under "Assurance" and "Transfiguration," perhaps inspired by Luke 9:23, where Jesus tells his disciples, "If anyone desires to come after me, let him deny himself, and take up his cross daily, and follow me." The key word comes from the Greek *akaloutheo,* "follow, accompany, follow as disciples." In this driving-gospel selection, Douroux recently instructed an audience of musicians to "take the tempo as a stately, consistent, Sunday morning processional as one following Jesus." The tempo suggested here is the quarter note = 58, whereas the even eighth notes moving under the vocal parts (eighth note = 116) are consistent. Clearly missing from the score is the typical "walking-bass" that undergirds and supports the vocal parts idiomatic of this traditional style of gospel music.

I have provided, for your consideration, a simplified example of what would be a most likely and commonly performed accompaniment with this composition. (See Figure 6.2) Note that, again, the tenor is played in the right hand creating a triad with the arpeggiated chordal accompaniment played in the left hand, ideally, in octaves.

No Trouble at the River

Finally, "No Trouble at the River," a contemporary spiritual, inspired by Joshua 3:15–17:

> ... and as those who bore the ark came to the Jordan, and the feet of the priests who bore the ark dipped in the edge of the water (for the Jordan overflows all its banks during the whole time of harvest), (16) that the waters which came down from upstream stood still, and rose in a heap very far way at Adam, the city that is beside Zaretan. So the water that went down into the Sea of the Arabah, the Salt Sea, failed, and were cut off; and the people crossed over opposite Jericho. (17) Then the priests who bore the ark of the covenant of the Lord stood firm on dry ground in the midst of the Jordan; and all Israel crossed over on dry ground, until all the people had crossed completely over the Jordan.

This Hebrew Bible reference is used to illustrate the challenges, anticipation, anxiety, and fear of crossing the Jordan River. Jordan, a popular name in the Negro spiritual, is used as a place, a river, as dividing line between time and eternity or between slave land and free land; a river chilly and cold that cannot stand still.[1] Therefore, the mood and character of this selection is contemplative, grave, serious, solemn, reflective, and weighty. This is reflected in the tempo (the quarter note = 40, or the eighth note = 80). The cue notes in the first measure provide brief introductory material most commonly associated with this selection. The constant dotted eighth followed by the sixteenth rhythm throughout the piece should always be unalterable and deliberately executed.

Since the understanding of the spirituals and the pleasure of singing them are increased by knowledge of the dialect in which the texts were composed, a suggestion or two about it will not be out of place. An error that confused many people is the idea that Negro dialect is uniform and fixed. "The idioms and pronunciations of the dialect vary in different sections of the South" explained James Weldon Johnson who made this very helpful observation:

> The first thing to remember is that the dialect is fundamentally English.
>
> An American from any part of the United States or an Englishman can, with not more than slight difficulty, understand it when it is spoken. The trouble comes in trying to get it from the print page. There are some idioms that may be strange, but they are few. The next thing to remember is that the pronunciation of the dialect is the result of the clision of the Negro, as far as possible, of all troublesome consonants and sound combinations.
>
> Thus: "th" as in "that" or "than" becomes "d" while "th" as in "thick" or "thin" becomes "t." This rule holds good at the end as well as at the beginning of wordsand syllables... Perhaps the most common mistake made in imitating Negro dialect is in giving to "de," the dialect for "the," the unvarying pronunciation of "dee."

It is pronounced "dee" when it precedes words beginning with a vowel sound, and "duh" before those beginning with a consonant sound. In this it follows the rule for the article "the."[2]

Figure 6.3

No Trouble at the River

Text: Margaret Pleasant Douroux, b.1941
Tune: Margaret Pleasant Douroux, b.1941
© Rev. Earl Pleasant Publising Co. Used by permission.

Excerpt from
New Wine in Old Wineskins
A Contemporary Congregational Song Supplement
GIA Publications, Inc. G-7113
Used by permission.

Therefore, in "No Trouble at the River," I recommend dropping the "t" from "don't" and "want" throughout. Again, remember that Dr. Douroux refers to this as a "contemporary" spiritual, one that has been composed in the style of a traditional folk spiritual but not a traditional or historical folk spiritual.

The only suggestion that I offer here for the accompaniment is much like that of the previous compositions. Playing the tenor with the treble voices in the right hand and the bass two octaves lower on the first and third beat of each measure adds sufficient accompaniment without over "gospelizing" this selection. There are cue notes at cadence points which should be doubled an octave lower. (See Figure 6.3)

Douroux's parents, Olga W. Pleasant and the late Earl A. Pleasant (renowned pastor and evangelist for whom Douroux's gospel music publishing company is named), are both legendary achievers in gospel music. Douroux has written more than 150 original copyrighted compositions and conducts workshops across the country and abroad. "The 98th Psalm is my testimony," she explained, and "My commitment to the work has to be because the Lord has done marvelous things, and because He has been consistently faithful . . . He has done more for me than I have done for myself." For more information, contact www.hmfgospel.org/dr.htm. *New Wine in Old Wineskins: A Contemporary Song Supplement* is available from GIA Publications by calling toll-free 1(800) 442-1358 or online at www.giamusic.com.

Notes

1. See "The Agencies and Models of Transformation" (Chapter 18) in James Lovell, Jr.'s unparalleled classic, *Black Song: The Forge and the Flame: The Story of How the Afro-American Spiritual Was Hammered Out.* (New York: Paragon House Publishers, 1972, 1986), pp.144–273.
2. James Weldon Johnson and J. Rosamond Johnson. *The Books of American Negro Spirituals.* (New York: Viking Press, 1925, 1926, 1953), pp. 44–45. I highly recommend J. Weldon Johnson's essay for a complete understanding of dialect and performance practices of spirituals.

Chapter

7

Contemporary Congregational Songs by V. Michael McKay

For more than a quarter of a century, churches throughout the country have been inspired by the words and music of V. Michael McKay. As a well-respected gospel music conductor, clinician, speaker, songwriter, and author, McKay has dedicated his life to a greater level of music ministry with a passion to meet the needs of the people in the contemporary Christian community. He stresses the importance of biblically-based text with a contemporary music idiom that encourages the congregation to participate fully in music throughout the service.

McKay (b. 1952) is a two-time Dove Award winner and a 2000 inductee into the Gospel Hall of Fame. National artists such as Yolanda Adams, Tramaine Hawkins, Darryl Coley, and Albertina Walker have recorded his songs. His compositions, "The Redeemed Praise" (#8), "In His Place" (#10), and "The Decision" (#63), first appeared in *For the Living of These Days: Resources for Enriching Worship* published in 1995 by Smyth & Helwys Publishing, Inc., Macon, GA. In addition to "The Decision" (#388), four other compositions, "The Lamb" (#179), "A Perfect Sacrifice" (#229), "Welcome to My Father's House" (#340), and "Koinonia" (#579) can be found in the *African American Heritage*

Contemporary Congregational Songs by V. Michael McKay
Originally published in a slightly different form in *The Hymn: A Journal of Congregational Song* 58, no. 4 (2007): 52–56. Used by permission. All rights reserved.

Hymnal published by GIA Publications. "Koinonia" also appears in *Gather Comprehensive* published by GIA Publications (#606), a hymnal and service book for Roman Catholic parishes in the United States since the Second Vatican Council. Additionally, it is included in the most recently published *Zion Still Sings: For Every Generation* published by Abingdon Press (#89), a revision of *Songs of Zion,* a supplemental worship resource for African American congregations in the United Methodist Church.

McKay was music director of "The Church Without Walls—Brookhollow Baptist Church" in Houston, TX when he composed "Koinonia." (See Figure 7.1) The Reverend Dr. Ralph D. West, Pastor/Founder called him late one Friday evening and asked him to write a composition for a group of college students who were meeting at the church the next morning. While he apologized for asking him to compose a song at the last minute, which was not an unusual request, he was confident that Michael would come through with just the right song, and that he did. The composition was so well received that he asked that it be taught and sung on the following Sunday morning for the fellowship period. The congregation was so moved by the text and the gesture of fellowship, so much so, that it continues to be sung there and in many churches across the nation today. I have used "Koinonia" in Australia, Canada, Brazil, in many church music workshops, and in college and university chapel services throughout the United States, and it never ceases to amaze me how people are brought together and led into an authentic fellowship experience in worship through music.

"Koinonia" is a Greek word meaning *fellowship.* In an age of overwhelming praise and worship songs and endless vertical texts, to God and from God, it is refreshing and welcoming to hear congregations sing this simple, yet profound horizontal text while shaking hands, embracing, and singing to each other. The text is:

How can I say that I love the Lord whom I've never,
ever seen before;
And forget to say that I love the one whom I walk beside
each and every day?
How can I look upon your face and ignore God's love?
You I must embrace!
You're my brother; you're my sister;
and I love you with the love of my Lord.

Figure 7.1

Koinonia

Figure 7.1, continued

"Koinonia" is usually sung in unison by the congregation and/or in three-parts with sopranos singing the top note of the treble voices, altos singing the middle note, and tenors singing the lowest note. On those wonderful occasions where there are basses present, I teach the part from the accompaniment. I suggest that the note in bass clef be occasionally played an octave lower and in octaves on the dotted quarter notes for a stronger and fuller accompaniment. A good tempo for "Koinonia" is the dotted quarter = ca. 66–69. The song is usually sung three or more times until community is created and the period of fellowship draws to a close.

However, I must caution that it should never be endlessly repeated until it becomes "annoyonia" for the congregation!

"The Lamb" (see Figure 7.2) is another contemporary congregational song by McKay found in the *African American Heritage Hymnal* (#179) that is often used for Easter, praise and worship repertoire, and as a final selection after communion. McKay shared his inspiration for "The Lamb" with me. "One of the greatest preachers of all times," he says, "is The Reverend Dr. A. Louis Patterson of Houston, TX. I often heard him, in that husky, deep voice, repeat the phrase 'Hallelujah to the Lamb' while he was preaching which inspired this text. I also included other phrases like—'Holy is the Lamb . . . ,' 'Worthy is the Lamb . . . ,' 'Jesus, You're the Lamb . . . ,' and occasionally, I improvise other verses like 'We Worship You, O Lamb of God' and 'We Praise You, O Lamb of God,' etc."

"The Lamb" is cyclical and easily adapted by congregations. Notice that word "Lamb" is always held for a full beat, which is tied to the last sixteenth note of the second beat, and should be performed with a slight crescendo. There are obvious places when the bass could and should be played an octave lower.

The syncopated rhythms are extremely important to the overall character of this piece and should never be rushed or clipped. They are sung much easier when they are kept in steady tempo. McKay gives the metronomic marking (the quarter note = 58) at the beginning of the piece. Like "Koinonia," the song can be sung in unison by the congregation and in three parts by the choir with sopranos singing the top note of the treble voices, altos singing the middle note, and tenors singing the lowest note. Again, the bass note must be adapted from the accompaniment. One important direction for "The Lamb" is that all four stanzas should be sung before the text "The perfect sacrifice You are." In other words, the double bar line at the end of the first page should be treated as a repeat sign to the beginning.

Both of these compositions and the three aforementioned compositions by McKay have been recorded by alumni and current students of the Morgan State University Choir of Baltimore (which I conducted with Joseph Joubert, pianist) and an instrumental ensemble that includes percussion, bass guitar, and Hammond Organ. The recordings are on the two double-disc CD sets entitled "49 Hidden Treasures from the *African*

American Heritage Hymnal"(CD-636) and "46 More Hidden Treasures from the *African American Heritage Hymnal*" (CD-711). They may be obtained through GIA Publications at www.giamusic.com or by calling toll-free 1 (800) 442-1358. These recordings provide very helpful performance practices and options for these and other selections in the *African American Heritage Hymnal.*

V. Michael McKay studied music at both Southern University in Baton Rouge, Louisiana and Texas Southern University in Houston. He now resides in Houston, TX. McKay's music is published through Schaff Music Publishing and GIA Publications, Inc. For further information about the music of V. Michael McKay, you may contact Schaff Music Publishing Company, LLC, P. O. Box 17923, Sugarland, TX 77496, (832) 578-9849 or online at www.vmichaelmckay.com/schaff.html.

Figure 7.2

The Lamb

Figure 7.2, continued

JESUS CHRIST

The per-fect sac-ri-fice You are. The

great-est gift in life by far. In

hum-ble grat-i-tude I come. Hal-le-

lu-jah to the Lamb of God.

Text: V. Michael McKay
Tune: V. Michael McKay
© Schaff Music Publishing
Used by permission.

Pastoral Considerations
and Worship Resources

Chapter

8

Pastoral Responsibility in the Music and Worship of the Church

C. Eric Lincoln and Lawrence Mamiya wrote in *The Black Church in the African American Experience* (1990): "In the Black Church good preaching and good singing are almost invariably the minimum conditions of a successful ministry." Unfortunately, in many African American churches today, the preaching and singing are prepared in isolation of, and even in competition with, each other. The concern seems to be who will "get the house," "dump the crowd," or make people shout—and not who will lead the congregation to a more profound and authentic alleluia.

Too often pastors and congregations seek and recruit charismatic "artists" with great musical gifts and résumés. We give them the sole responsibility of the music only to discover that they lack knowledge of the essential characteristics of a true music ministry. The recurring result is an offering that is out of focus with what the needs and understanding of the congregation ought to be.

In his essay "Church Music: A Position Paper," the late Dr. Wendell P. Whalum unyieldingly declared:

There is probably no area of Black church life more perplexing and pathetic than music and what we have let happen to it. Not only have a conglomerate of styles and functions crept into our church music, but there seems to be little knowledge of the "why music in worship" concept in the minds of those whose responsibility it is to govern the church and its music. The pathetic aspect is that the music, often enjoyed by worshipers, offers little by way of Christian education or kingdom building, and the effects last only a few minutes after its "embers" fade away.

…As I see it, the clergy and the musicians are to be blamed for what has occurred, and logically, it is their responsibility to correct it. Some of the blame, too, will inevitably point to many of us who, in addition to being practicing church musicians, also have, little by little, abdicated our responsibility of instructing those who have not had good solid training but who, for various reasons, assume the task of musical leadership. We are, therefore, guilty of standing by, through the years, watching music in the Black church, to a large degree, deteriorate and, to some extent, decay.[1]

This stinging indictment challenges me to attempt to empower and inspire pastors to take a fundamental role in the music and worship in the church. This nonnegotiable should not be confused with the pastor as "micromanager," as in many churches where the pastor alone makes too many decisions about music and worship. A well-balanced relationship between the pastor and the minister of music will produce a more cohesive worship experience.

Whalum further cites situations that should definitely be avoided:

Members of the clergy have sometimes been, or are guilty of misusing the music portions of the church program. Usually without even good layman's ability to appreciate music, they impose inferior standards, for various reasons, on their congregations. Hymn books of good, solid reference are lacking and choirs are formed as fund-raising organizations rather than for the purpose that they should serve. Afraid of cost, many ministers have selected instruments for their church houses, organs, and pianos without any knowledge of quality needs. Too, as a money-saving gimmick, the minister will often hire a musician who will accept a nominal fee, but who knows nothing of standard literature or choir training, and all too frequently such musicians do not even know any of the history of the Black church.[2]

Conversely, there are musicians who oppose the pastor's involvement in the music ministry because as trained, skilled, and gifted leaders of music they feel they should have charge over the music department and what should and should not be presented in worship. It is this type of egocentric attitude that has sustained and fortified much of the unbalanced, unfocused, unbiblical, and nontheological music offerings that many churches have become addicted to or made to endure.

Consider 1 Chronicles 15: "David ordered the heads of Levites to assign their relatives to sing in the choir, accompanied by a well-equipped marching band, and fill the air with joyful sound," and "Kenaniah, the Levite in charge of music, a very gifted musician, was music director."[3] It is clear that David was the "pastor." David appointed Kenaniah because he was skilled in singing and song, but Kenaniah understood that he was still accountable to David, who had appointed him.

Unfortunately, in many churches, the pastor is excluded or does not participate in the process of selecting the director or minister of music. Nothing could be more dangerous and conflicting for the fruitful partnership that must be established and maintained between the pastor and the musician.

Too many musicians do not understand the church and its history, the denomination and its doctrine and theology, the liturgy, worship, and appropriate sacred music literature. Instead, they make arbitrary and isolated weekly decisions about what the congregation will hear. This is where the pastor must assume the role of teacher and supervisor for the musician whose skills will not substitute for a lack of biblical, theological, and pastoral understanding.

Be clear: There are pastors who possess neither the ability to sing nor to play, but that does not exclude them from the decision making relative to worship. Too often, ministers allow bad theology to be taught in rehearsal and sung in worship because the people seem to like it and respond by shouting. Ideally, pastors and musicians should plan worship together; in that way, the musician will always operate in harmony with the Word, and the pastor will not feel that he or she is in competition with the music.

At Shaw University Divinity School, I taught my students not only to select pre-sermon hymns that supported their sermons, but also to select an invitational hymn that would reinforce and empower their message. Many of them discovered when reading the texts of the hymns in class that this was something that they should be doing in their individual churches. Although they were unable to play or sing the tunes, they were qualified to determine what text was appropriate for worship. More importantly, they understood that it was the primary responsibility of the musical leadership to produce what they had selected. Their input became essential to the planning of worship.

I have heard many pastors lament that they sing only a few hymns because the congregation knows only a few. It is the responsibility of the musician, in consultation with the pastor, to broaden and expand the hymnody of the church. Unfortunately, many churches have talented but untrained musicians who cannot read music and make no effort to learn. Therefore, the choir and congregation are held hostage to the limitations of those musicians and must accept what is offered.

Let me reiterate: Pastors must take responsibility for what is being rendered in the presence of the people of God. The truth is that there are many fine musicians who have studied music, but have not studied the church. They are musicians who work in churches, but they are not necessarily church musicians. They are guilty of selecting music that has been professionally recorded, commercially marketed, and distributed without biblical or theological insight concerning its appropriateness for the worship service of God's people. Whatever sells on the radio or TV becomes the repertoire for the church. When this happens, the pastor is in large part at fault.

Several years ago, I was invited to a meeting of three of the largest music publishers in New York City. During a discussion about sacred music—more specifically, about gospel music—a question was raised about a very popular song having biblical and theological inconsistencies and flaws. The immediate response was, "We aren't pastors or theologians, and we are only concerned about what sells! If you can write a hit song that has all of those elements, that's great, but the bottom line for us is, does it sell?"

Unfortunately, the selection of music and worship styles in many of our churches is being dictated by the mass media and record companies who are not trying to win souls to Christ, but are merely selling music to consumers. Pastors must be aware of this practice and the commercial conspiracy that has invaded many of our churches.

So, what's a pastor to do? Here are some beginning steps; more will be said in future articles. First, the pastor must set aside time to think about worship for his or her church. This will mean reading books and referencing the web for worship information. Second, after the pastor has determined the worship approach needed for the congregation, he or she should ask the minister of music to do the same. Third, the two must come together to develop a "worship portfolio" for the church. Prayer will reinforce the priority of glorifying God in worship. Although this meeting will not etch things in stone, it will give strong direction. Finally, this meeting should be followed by regular meetings that allow the leadership to evaluate the past and plan for future worship experiences. Coming together allows interaction, critique, compliments, and challenges to be presented in an environment that provides growth. The meetings should always begin with the positive aspects of the worship service, move to constructive evaluation, and then review the negative aspects (which should be termed and seen as "growth opportunities").

Pastors and musicians owe it to their congregation—the people who pay their salaries—to meet regularly and plan for the gathering on the Lord's Day.[4] And it must be the pastor who leads and guides the minister of music along this road less traveled!

Notes

1. Wendell P. Whalum. "Church Music: A Position Paper (with special consideration of music in the Black church)" in *Readings in African American Church Music and Worship*, James Abbington, ed. (Chicago: GIA Publications, 2001), 503.
2. Ibid., 504.
3. 1 Chronicles 15:16,22, *The Message.*
4. James Abbington. *Let Mt. Zion Rejoice! Music in the African American Church* (Valley Forge, PA: 2001), 29.

Chapter

9

Nonmusical Considerations for the Church Musician

In 1988, C. Harry Causey published a book entitled *Things They Didn't Tell Me About Being a Minister of Music* (Music Revelation, 1988). This book takes a humorous look at some serious topics every church musician needs to understand. The chapters are entitled:

"They Didn't Tell Me I Would Have to Be a Politician"
"…Married to the Job"
"…a Financial Wizard"
"…a Psychologist"
"…a Producer"
"…a Bible Scholar"
"…a Servant"
"…an Administrator"
"…a Personality"
"…a Disciplinarian"

At the time this book was published, there were few, if any, resources that focused on the nonmusical attributes of music leadership in the church. Causey's writing was witty, practical, inspirational, and challenging to me as a young minister of music at a very large urban congregation in Detroit.

Nonmusical Considerations for the Church Musician
Originally published in a slightly different form in *The Musician's Walk: An Ethical Labyrinth*, ed. James Jordan (Chicago: GIA Publications, Inc., 2006), 255–73. All rights reserved.

In 1994, Robin Knowles Wallace wrote a similar book expanding on Causey's position entitled *Things They Never Tell You Before You Say "Yes"* (Abingdon Press, 1994).

As a music minister, I quickly discovered there were many nonmusical considerations, duties, responsibilities, and unspoken expectations that went above and beyond my musical preparation and training. For example, it was one thing to identify members of the choir as either soprano, alto, tenor, or bass, but it was another thing to know their names and be able to address them as individuals.

The first and foremost requirement of a church musician is to love the Lord God with all one's heart and mind. If musicians do not first love God and the people of God, then all their talents, skills, and training will not help them to succeed.[1] Although this seems basic and simple, musicians often talk church talk but refuse to walk church walk. Just as ministers are called of God, so, too, church musicians are called of God. There is a major distinction between a *musician who works in a church* and a *church musician.*

James Robert Davidson defines a minister of music as "the person who combines the tasks of ministry and music leadership...and is often ordained to the ministry with music as the tool of his [or her] calling. This role includes the gathering of the people, the teaching of them, and the caring for them through a musical dimension within the total redemptive-creativity activity." He explains that the term "is relatively recent to church music having appeared around the mid-twentieth century among evangelical Protestant churches in America. A real impetus toward its use came from the Southern Baptist Convention with its establishment of the Department of Church Music (1941) as a part of the Sunday School Board and its implementation of Schools of Church Music in the various seminaries." An even more important difference, says Davidson, is that

> unlike the director of music, the minister of music is involved with more than simply choral and instrumental ensembles and leading the congregational singing. He [or she] is concerned with the total congregation, what the needs are of the congregation as individuals, and what music will best meet the needs, and effect a desired response. Through his [or her] choice and use of music, he [or she] is involved in

the process of instilling theological concepts as well as a devotional vocabulary. His [or her] ability to know his [or her] congregation and individual attitudes, to identify with these, and to provide the catalyst for a feeling of community in the proclamation of Christian truth through music compromise the discipline and limits of his [or her] work.[2]

Although this definition does not reflect what many ministers of music do, it is certainly a herculean model to which we can all aspire.

This chapter will focus on nonmusical issues and considerations for the church choir director, many of which violate simple and basic moral, ethical, spiritual, and professional conduct. Topics range from illegally photocopying music; to criticizing, disrobing, and dismantling the musical work of other choirs and their directors; to refusing to work with pastors and other ministerial staff associated with worship leadership.

Photocopying Music

Almost without fail, the first page of every copy of music has a copyright date and a statement such as: "Photocopying of this publication without permission of the publisher is a violation of the U.S. Code of Law for which the responsible individual or institution is subject to criminal prosecution. No one is exempt," or other similar language. A complete copy of the United States Copyright Law and further information regarding the copyright law may be obtained online at the U.S. Copyright Office Web site (www.copyright.gov), or by writing The U.S. Copyright Office, Library of Congress, Washington, DC 20559.

It is important to know that you can request permission to make photocopies of copyrighted music by securing licenses from the copyright owner prior to making any of the copies. You can also obtain permission to use many congregationally sung compositions by contacting the applicable licensing agency, such as OneLicense.net. They can be reached at www. onelicense.net, by calling (800) 663-1501, or by writing 7343 S. Mason Avenue, Chicago, IL 60638. Another such licensing agency is Christian Copyright Licensing, Inc. (CCLI), www.ccli.com. It is important to know that a reprint license *does not* grant the right to photocopy or duplicate any choral music, cantatas, musicals, handbell music, keyboard arrangements, vocal solos, or instrumental works. The license grants duplicating rights for congregational music only.

The law provides for the owner of a copyright to recover damages ranging from $500 to $100,000 per copyright infringed. If willful infringement for commercial advantages and private financial gain is proven, then criminal fines of up to $250,000 and/or a five-year prison sentence may apply—not worth the risk to the musician or the church!

What many do not seem to realize is that photocopying and then replacing those copies is much more expensive than purchasing the original scores. Plus, people tend to value an original piece of music with more pride and care. The excuses, which are many, are all inappropriate, unjustifiable, and do not exempt the musician or the church from the copyright laws:

- Our budget does not include money for sheet music.
- We have a very limited budget.
- The people will only lose the music.
- Music is too expensive.
- We sing too much music to purchase every composition that we sing.

There are acceptable ways of dealing with these types of issues rather than perpetuating the problem of continually photocopying and distributing music for performance. There are times, however, when permission may be granted to photocopy a piece of music:

- When a composition is permanently out of print and copies are no longer available, a publisher may grant permission for a limited number of copies to be made.
- When a composition is on backorder, a publisher may grant the director permission to photocopy the composition with the understanding that the photocopies will be destroyed and no longer used when the originals arrive.

Choir directors and members are taught to meticulously observe the correct notes, dynamics, accidentals, texts, and tempos, but disregarding the copyright on the printed music from which the choir sings is impermissible and inexcusable.

Lack of Preparation for Rehearsals

Another nonmusical issue choir directors face, although they are made aware of it and are evaluated consistently in their formal training, is not being sufficiently prepared for rehearsals. For example, choir directors themselves are often tardy for rehearsal, although they reprimand their members for tardiness. It is not uncommon for choir members to wait as long as fifteen or twenty minutes for the choir director to begin rehearsal, without notice, apology, or explanation from the director. Unfortunately, many directors wait until the last minute to make preparations for rehearsal because they consider it a low priority. This is apparent when sheet music is not in place or arranged for members upon their arrival, no repertoire schedule is posted or available, or choir members are asked what they would like to sing. Nothing could be more frustrating, insulting, and inconsiderate to the volunteer church choir members who willingly give their time and talents on a regular basis.

If one assumes the duties and responsibilities of choir director, then there is no excuse for such conduct and lack of commitment. Such behavior illustrates a lackadaisical and carefree attitude toward the organization and its mission, which makes it difficult to demand excellence of the choir. As director, you must lead by example!

There are a plethora of resources available to assist and guide choir directors in effective rehearsal planning and preparation, including musical resources, methods, vocal and instrumental literature in all styles and genres, videos, CDs, DVDs, and online instruction, which makes it impossible for a choir director to be unprepared. No conscientious, seriously committed, open-minded director can afford to ignore the many valuable resources that are available. To be certain, there are varying levels of quality and reliability, so we must sort through them to determine what is most useful and helpful to each of us.

Various Levels of Musicianship, Personality, and Commitment

This brings me to a very sensitive issue: *musical* and *nonmusical* as it relates to musicians. Today, many churches and institutions are the unfortunate hostages of various levels of musicianship, personality, and commitment—and, as a choir director, that is challenging. In 1985, the late Wendell P. Whalum identified five categories of problematic music personnel serving in many churches.

Category 1. *Talented but untrained musicians:* These musicians often cannot read music, have no knowledge of choir organization or choral directing, and have no awareness of the historical importance of the hymns, liturgy, or religious service.

Category 2. *Untrained and untalented but willing musicians:* This group, larger in number than one would suspect, is made up of people who have had one or two years of piano study and are willing to accept leadership because no one in the church will or can assume responsibility for the music.

Category 3. *Musicians with basic music training who accept church music duties without understanding what the program should be about and how it should be conducted:* The result is that much of what is offered is out of focus with the needs and understanding of the congregation.

Category 4. *Musicians with good training and previous exposure to excellent music who ignore the level of the congregation:* Instead of educating the congregation, these musicians operate on a plane too sophisticated for the congregation. These musicians will frequently impose oratorios, cantatas, and pageants on people not yet educated in hymns and anthems who are, therefore, not ready for extended works.

Category 5. *Musicians with excellent training who assume an attitude of superiority and make no attempt to lift [or broaden] the level of musical awareness:* This kind of musician is usually identified as the organist-director who will officiate only at Sunday morning services or at the funerals and weddings of prominent citizens of the community.[3]

As painful and realistic as Whalum's categories are, they deserve our attention and consideration. In my career as a church and university choir director, my actions have put me into several of these categories, for which I have had to confess, repent, and "turn from my wicked ways."

I have been guilty of choosing music for the choir and congregation based on what I thought was appropriate to my training, my musical experience, my personal taste, and my understanding of "proper" liturgy and sacred music literature. My choices, however, did not take into consideration the people I was leading and serving or their culture, and often grossly failed to meet the needs of the worshipers or the worship service. Of course, I justified my decisions by insisting that I was committed to "lifting," "raising," and "elevating" the musical standards, which was a very narrow, prejudiced, and *vertical* choice of vocabulary and attitude. I have since learned that a *horizontal* vocabulary, which includes "augmenting," "expanding," "extending," and "increasing" the musical experiences and exposure, is much more appropriate, admirable, and pleasing to God.

We cannot adequately serve people we do not know or consider essential when planning music for the choir or congregation. The selection of music must not represent a personality, another church or choir, or a standard set by some outside group or organization; rather, the people must understand the text and the music to the extent that it becomes incarnate in their lives and guides them through life's joys and challenges.

If we are to sing and pray (often at the same time) with spirit and understanding, then we must mean what we say and know what we mean. S. Paul Schilling once said, "Unless the hymns we use in worship express our convictions, we might as well sing the stock market reports, the real estate ads from the daily newspaper, or a list of names from the telephone directory."[4] The same holds true for anthems and arranged hymns and spirituals. Hymns and choral repertoire should become more than a group of songs and compositions that a choir and congregation have mastered and regularly performed. They should, as James Robert Davidson asserts, "instill the theological concepts as well as a devotional vocabulary which provide the catalyst for a feeling of community [and understanding] in the proclamation of Christian truth through music."

I have also been guilty of imposing cantatas and other extended works on my choirs and congregations who needed a more diverse and inclusive hymnody, as well as an appreciation and understanding of anthems. One of the most important duties and responsibilities of the music director is to *educate* the congregation musically by teaching, illustrating, and providing a clear understanding of what is being sung and played in the church. It is insensitive to make no attempt to determine the level of the choir and congregation while steadily inflicting a personal musical agenda or the taste of music preferred by a few on all.

Finally, I have also been guilty of asking who the deceased is or who is getting married before checking my availability to serve as organist for a funeral or wedding. I now see these as moral and ethical violations of my walk and my responsibility as a "minister of music" and a church musician.

Loyalty and Allegiance to the Musician

Equally as sensitive in our walk is the unspoken need and expectation of loyalty, allegiance, and obligation from choir members above and beyond the expectations of the organization and its mission. It is unfortunate when a choir director's egocentric, narcissistic, and self-indulgent personality, insecurities, and psychological needs impose an unspoken but implicit loyalty, faithfulness, and allegiance on the choir members. I know choir directors who act as if they "own" their members, boasting of their loyalty to them even against the church leadership and other choirs and musicians. The need to control and manipulate people is dangerous and demands a serious revisiting of the calling of choir director or music director.

In some churches, the choir director's influence and decisions extend far beyond the realm of pastoral leadership. This is also often true in institutions where musical leadership has not changed for many years.

The tendency is to feel a certain loyalty to the *person* without considering what is best or right for the church or institution. This type of behavior manifests itself by constantly being critical of and dismantling the work of other musicians, choirs, and musical organizations. The director constantly criticizes, finds fault, and attempts to destroy the work of others to elevate himself/herself. Eventually, the choir takes on the personality and superiority of the director and joins in the destruction. This is very prevalent, habitual, and typical of churches that have more than one choir or are considered one of the few outstanding choirs in the community and feel the need to diminish the others.

Using this unspoken influence, choir directors are able to convince members of their choir not the sing with other groups or participate in musical activities sponsored by other directors or groups. Members feel it is "unfaithful and unloyal" to cross the picket line established by their director. There are instances, perpetuated by musicians, where members are forbidden to attend worship services other than those at which they sing.

Such immoral, unethical, unprofessional, and childish behavior should be forbidden, discouraged, and not tolerated by church musicians. It is destructive, disconcerting, contemptuous, cynical, and violates every principle of Christianity. These are very unfortunate nonmusical considerations for church musicians that are alive and well in churches all over North America.

The Relationship between Pastor and Musician

"It will remain bad theology so long as the theologian and the artist refuse to communicate with one another, as long as the theologian regards the artist as fundamentally a temperamental trifler, and the theologian as an obstinate and ignorant theorist, the best we shall get is patronage from church to music, together with tentative moralisms from musicians to musicians," Erik Routley wrote in his classic *Church Music and Theology*. "At worst it will be, as it often in practice is, a wicked waste of an opportunity of glorifying God through fruitful partnership."[5] If we substitute the word *pastor*, *minister*, or *priest* for "theologian" and the term *musician, minister of music, director of music*, or *choir director* for "artist," Routley's statement becomes more relevant and applicable.

It is unfortunate when a pastor and musician cannot and will not work together in a church. Few give little if any time to developing a strong and fruitful partnership. In some churches, the tension between pastor and musician is distracting and becomes the focus of the worship. This lack of communication, cooperation, and partnership leads to many distracted, disengaged, and meaningless worship experiences. Routley best called it a "wicked waste"! Successful partnerships begin with understanding, and productive partnerships rely on quality communication. Many people confuse talking with communicating. People think that the more they talk, the better they are communicating. But good communication begins when we stop talking and listen. Much of the time, we can improve our communication skills by listening more. "Talking at people," writes N. Lee Orr, "means we not only miss what they are saying but also risk misunderstanding their point of view. We then leave the encounter further convinced of how right we are, which hardens our position."[6] It is no wonder the other person is not enthusiastic or optimistic about future dialogue.

Orr continues, "Working partnerships between ministers and musicians result when both parties actively support the other, avoid public criticism of the other, ignore minor irritants, and work toward building a friendship."[7]

Pastors and musicians need to possess a rudimentary knowledge of the suppositions, skills, and vocabulary of each other's discipline. Without this knowledge, communication and partnership become difficult or even impossible, and even the best-intentioned efforts at collaborative ministry become strained.[8] "Clergy who have had excellent instruction in pastoral care often lack any sense of how to converse in a professional way with one of the single most important colleagues in their ministry: the church musician." Carol Doran and Thomas Troeger continue, "The story works in reverse as well: the musician, inexperienced in discussing theology and often feeling powerless, is fearful of beginning a conversation with the pastor about the way music functions in the liturgy. Sometimes musicians view their contributions entirely from the perspective of performance without considering how it fits with the liturgical and pastoral needs of the congregation."[9]

It is impossible for church musicians to develop, fortify, perpetuate, and strengthen their *walk* if they are not willing to walk with those to whom they are accountable and responsible. While it seems that protocol would make the pastor responsible for forging and establishing a partnership, it may be that the musicians should take the path less traveled and initiate the communication and partnership. The work of the Kingdom is so much greater than our egos, idiosyncrasies, agendas, and pride.

Conclusion

Finally, the soul, the spirit, and the walk of the musician should be so visible, genuine, unpretentious, sincere, and truly incarnate in the total life of the musician that it serves as a model for all. I hasten to add that this is not to assume we as musicians are perfect, free from sin, and never tempted by the tsunamis, hurricanes, earthquakes, and wildfires of life. However, we cannot lead where we have not been. We cannot teach what we do not know. We cannot show the way to where we have never been. And we cannot talk of experiences we have never had. While many of these nonmusical considerations are blunt, candid, direct, head-on, point-blank, straightforward, and create a sense of discomfort, it is certainly not my intention to "tear down" but rather my hope and objective to "build up" for the Kingdom and Glory of God!

Notes

1. James Abbington, *Let Mt. Zion Rejoice! Music in the African American Church* (Valley Forge, PA: Judson Press, 2001), 15.
2. James Robert Davidson, *A Dictionary of Protestant Church Music* (Metuchen, NJ: Scarecrow, 1975), 205–06.
3. The list is paraphrased from Wendell P. Whalum, "Music in the Churches of Black Americans: A Critical Statement," *The Black Perspective in Music* 14, no. 1 (Winter 1986), 16–7. This article also appears in *Readings in African American Church Music and Worship,* edited by James Abbington (Chicago: GIA, 2001), 503–04.

4. S. Paul Schilling, *The Faith We Sing* (Philadelphia, PA: Westminster, 1983), 23.

5. Erik Routley, *Church Music and Theology* (Philadelphia, PA: Muhlenberg, 1959), 110.

6. N. Lee Orr, *The Church Music Handbook for Pastors and Musicians* (Nashville, TN: Abingdon, 1991), 54.

7. Ibid., 67–70.

8. Carol Doran and Thomas H. Troeger, *Trouble at the Table* (Nashville, TN: Abingdon, 1992), 79.

9. Ibid., 78–83.

Chapter

10

Worship Resources for Pastors and Musicians

One of the greatest tragedies attendant to many of our worship services is a lack of serious and effective planning. It is tragic when pastors and musicians do not plan worship together and or are improperly prepared to do so. In the book *African American Worship: New Eyes for Seeing*, Frederick H. Talbot says,

> "Two contemporary management planners have defined planning as 'deciding in advance *what* to do, *how* to do it, *when* to do it, and *who* is to do it.' The definition summarizes the essential elements in planning: *what*, *how*, *when*, and *who*. Planning bridges the gap from where we are to where we want to go. It makes it possible for things to occur which would not otherwise happen and although the best-laid plans can fail to materialize, without some form of planning events are left to chance. Experience shows that nothing significant happens when left to chance. In fact, the dictum rings true: 'to fail to plan is to plan to fail.' "[1]

Quite importantly, all pastors and musicians must consistently work together to plan worship services. The church can no longer afford rivalries

Worship Resources for Pastors and Musicians
Originally published in a slightly different form in *The National Baptist Voice*, Winter 2005, 46–47.
Used by permission. All rights reserved.

that pit pastors against musicians and vice-versa. Nor can the church continue offering worship that is disjointed and less uplifting because it is void of the partnering work of the pastor and the musician/minister of music.

"It will remain bad theology so long as the theologian and the artist refuse to communicate with one another, as long as the theologian regards the artist as fundamentally a temperamental trifler, and the theologian as an obstinate and ignorant theorist, the best we shall get is patronage from church to music, together with tentative moralisms from musicians to musicians," Erik Routley wrote in his classic, *Church Music and Theology.* "At worst it will be, as it often in practice is, a wicked waste of an opportunity for glorifying God through fruitful partnership."[2] And, if we substitute the word pastor, minister, or priest for "theologian" and the term musician or choir director for "artist," these comments are still relevant.

In addition, planning worship should not be sporadic, seasonal, or for convenience. It must be consistent and viewed as a sacred task. There must be sufficient time for the musician to select and prepare the choir for regular and special occasions in the life of the church. Worship planned in advanced will allow both the pastor and the musician to investigate, gather, and study relevant materials. Pastors and musicians must have weekly time set aside to plan all worship services. In addition to these weekly planning sessions, they should meet at least twice each year to review the church calendar and plan worship accordingly. The twice yearly sessions should occur in concert with other members of the church community.

In her book, *African American Christian Worship*, Dr. Melva Costen adds the following suggestions for worship,

1. Consider the lived experiences of worshipers and their understanding of worship.
2. Consider the worship space.
3. Become familiar with your denominational polity and theology of worship to determine what elements are required and what your denomination believes about each of the elements.
4. Use Scripture to undergird the entire worship event.
5. Consider the flow of the service to determine what pattern facilitates worship in the particular congregation.
6. Take care that the language of the liturgy is inclusive.[2]

Next, although it is essential to have a well-planned worship service, when the Holy Spirit shows up, the worship is subject to change by the One whom we worship. Dr. William Watley, pastor of St. James AME Church in Newark, NJ cautions, "We must be flexible in our worship and not get so caught up and upset about what is on the printed bulletin." He continues, "One Sunday at Saint James the Spirit fell, and it was obvious that it was preaching time. I called for the sermonic hymn and took my text. After the service, one of my anal-retentive, high-liturgical members came up to me and said, 'Reverend, you forgot to acknowledge the visitors and call for Sister So-and-So who had a presentation to make to the Building Fund.' I told her that I didn't forget but that when the Holy Ghost comes everything changes. Ever since that Sunday, at the top of our bulletin is the heading: 'The worship is under the direction of the Holy Spirit and subject to change without notice.' "[4]

In addition to partnering and planning, continuing education is needed. If a pastor, minister, or worship leader has had theological training in a seminary or divinity school, it is likely that neither music and worship nor liturgy were required in their course of study, if they were offered at all. The same can be said for musicians. If they have received formal training, it is very likely that courses in church music, hymnology, theology or music in worship were not required. Musicians earn degrees in applied vocal or instrumental performance, music education, choral conducting, etc. However, few are trained to understand the role of music in worship, liturgy, and biblical and theological music literature that is appropriate for the church. All of the former makes continuation education critical for pastors and musicians!

A part of continuing education is making use of resources. Fortunately, in the past two decades, there has been a tremendous increase in resources such as textbooks, hymnals, hymnal supplements, videos, CDs, cassettes, conferences and workshops. Even better, there are now resources for and by African Americans about their worship styles and their theologies of worship. The list at the end of this article contains a variety of resources that will help pastors and musicians develop a beginning worship library.

Although space only allows for a brief comment, I dare not conclude this article without mentioning the problem of worship as entertainment. A clear understanding of worship will greatly assist in pastors and musicians being keenly aware that the church is not a religious theater where performers are paid to amuse those who attend. It is an assembly of redeemed sinners—men and women called unto Christ and commissioned to spread His gospel to the ends of the earth. As A. W. Tozer said: "She [the Church] appears to have decided that if she cannot conquer the great god of Entertainment, she may as well join forces with him and make whatever use she can of his powers. . .The church that can't worship must be entertained. And men [and women] who can't lead a church to worship must provide the entertainment."[5] Clearly, the pastor and musician must be able to lead the church to worship or face the alternative.

The African American Lectionary is a resource tool that not only highlights the African American ecclesial traditions and moments that creatively express the joy, freedom, and the challenges of being both African American and Christian (e.g., Watch Night, African Heritage Sunday, Usher's Day, and Women's Day), but also recognizes the liturgical calendar celebrated across a variety of ecclesial traditions (e.g., Advent, Christmas, Lent, Easter, and Pentecost). By incorporating both the traditional moments of the lectionary cycle, as well as those moments of significance across many African American ecclesial traditions, the online Lectionary allows the user to creatively and comprehensively select material to create a program that will exactly fit your congregation's needs and expectations."[6]

By working together, planning, understanding the role of the Holy Spirit, and being continually educated, pastors and musicians will gain a wholistic and holy understanding of worship. The resources listed below, written and compiled by African American worship scholars, pastors, musicians, and professors, will prove helpful in providing worship principles and practical approaches that will enhance worship to the glory of God.

Selected Resources for African American Music and Worship

2007   Valerie Bridgeman Davis and Safiyah Fosua, *Companion to the Africana Worship Book*, (Nashville: Discipleship Resources).

2007   Valerie Bridgeman Davis and Safiyah Fosua, *The Africana Worship Book: Year B*, (Nashville: Discipleship Resources).

2007   Kathlyn Gay, *African American Holidays, Festivals, and Celebrations: The History, Customs, and Symbols associated with both Traditional and Contemporary Religious and Secular Events observed by Americans of African Descent* (Detroit: Omni graphics, Inc.).

2006   *Beams of Heaven: Hymns of Charles Albert Tindley (1851–1933)* edited by S. T. Kimbrough, Jr. and Carlton R. Young (New York: General Board of Global Ministries, The United Methodist Church).

2006   Valerie Bridgeman Davis and Safiyah Fosua, *The Africana Worship Book: Year A*, (Nashville: Discipleship Resources).

2006   Howard Thurman, *Essential Writings* (Maryknoll: New York: Orbis Books).

2005   Cheryl A. Kirk-Duggan, *More African American Special Days: 15 Complete Worship Services* (Nashville: Abingdon Press).

2005   Anne E. Streaty Wimberly, *Soul Stories: African American Christian Education*, (Nashville: Abingdon Press).

2004   Anne E. Streaty Wimberly, *Nurturing Faith and Hope: Black Worship as a Model for Christian Education* (Cleveland: Pilgrim Press).

2003   Cheryl A. Kirk-Duggan, *Soul Pearls: Worship Resources for the Black Church.* (Nashville: Abingdon Press).

2003   Cheryl A. Kirk-Duggan, *Mary Had a Baby: An Advent Study Based on African American Spirituals.* (Nashville: Abingdon Press).

2003   James Abbington and Linda H. Hollies, *Going to Wait! African American Church Worship Resources between Pentecost and Advent* (Chicago: GIA Publications).

2003   Linda H. Hollies, *Trumpet in Zion, Year C* (Cleveland: Pilgrim Press).

2003   Wyatt Tee Walker, *Spirits That Dwell in Deep Woods: The Prayer and Praise Hymns of the Black Religious Experience*, James Abbington, editor. (Chicago: GIA Publications).

2002   James Abbington and Linda H. Hollies, *Waiting to Go! African American Church Worship Resources from Advent through Pentecost* (GIA Publications).

2002   Linda H. Hollies, *Trumpet in Zion, Year B* (Cleveland: Pilgrim Press).

2001   James Abbington, *Let Mt. Zion Rejoice!* (Valley Forge, PA: Judson Press).

2001   James Abbington, *Readings in African American Church Music and Worship* (Chicago: GIA Publications, Inc.)

2001   Cheryl A. Kirk-Duggan, *The Undivided Soul: Helping Congregations Connect Body and Spirit.* (Nashville: Abingdon Press).

2001   Linda H. Hollies, *Trumpet in Zion: Worship Resources, Year A* (Cleveland: Pilgrim Press).

2000   Diana L. Hayes, *Were You There? Stations of the Cross.* (Maryknoll, NY: Orbis Books).

1997   Grenae D. Dudley and Carlyle F. Stewart III, *Sankofa: Celebrations for the African American Church.* (Cleveland: United Church Press).

1997   Gwendolin Sims Warren, *Ev'ry Time I Feel the Spirit: 101 Best-Loved Psalms, Gospel Hymns, and Spiritual Songs of the African American Church*, (New York: Henry Holt & Company).

1996   Cheryl A. Kirk-Duggan, *African American Special Days: 15 Complete Worship Services*. (Nashville: Abingdon Press).

1996   William Farley Smith, *Songs of Deliverance: Organ Arrangements and Congregational Acts of Worship for the Church Year Based on African American Spirituals*. (Nashville: Abingdon Press).

1994   James Melvin Washington, *Conversations with God: Two Centuries of Prayers by African Americans*. (New York: HarperCollins Publishers)

1990   Jon Michael Spencer, *Unsung Hymns by Black and Unknown Bards*. (Durham, NC: Duke University Press).

1990   William B. McClain, *Come Sunday: The Liturgy of Zion—A Companion to Songs of Zion* (Nashville: Abingdon Press).

Current Denominational Hymnals & Supplements

2007   National Association of Congregational Christian Churches (NACCC) *Hymns for a Pilgrim People*

2007   United Methodist Church (African American Congregations) *Zion Still Sings: For Every Generation*

2001   National Baptist Convention of America, Inc. (NBCA) *The New National Baptist Hymnal: 21st Century Hymnal*

2001   African American Protestant *African American Heritage Hymnal*

1999   Evangelical Lutheran Church in America and African American
        Congregations of the Lutheran Church – Missouri Synod
        This Far by Faith: An African American Resource for Worship

1996   African Methodist Episcopal Zion Church (AMEZ)
        The African Methodist Episcopal Zion Bicentennial Hymnal

1993   Episcopal Church
        Lift Every Voice and Sing II

1987   Roman Catholic
        Lead Me, Guide Me: The African American Catholic Hymnal

1987   Christian Methodist Episcopal Church (CME)
        The Hymnal of the Christian Methodist Episcopal Church

1984   African Methodist Episcopal Church (AME)
        AMEC Hymnal

1982   Progressive National Baptist Convention, Inc. (PNBC)
        The New Progressive National Baptist Hymnal

1982   Church of God in Christ (COGIC)
        Yes, Lord!

1981   United Methodist Church (African American Congregations)
        Songs of Zion

1977   Church of Christ (Holiness), USA
        His Fullness Songs, rev. ed

1966   Fire Baptized Holiness Church
        Hymnal of the F.B.H. Church

1961   National Baptist Convention, USA, Inc.   (NBCUSA)
        The Baptist Standard Hymnal with Responsive Readings

Recommended (Other Worship Resources)

2008   William H. Willimon, *A Guide to Preaching and Leading Worship*, (Louisville: Westminster John Knox Press).

2007   James Abbington, ed. *New Wine in Old Wineskins: A Contemporary Congregational Song Supplement*. (Chicago: GIA Publications, Inc).

2007   John L. Bell, *The Singing Thing Too: Enabling Congregations to Sing*. (Chicago: GIA Publications, Inc).

2006   Peter Busch and Christine O'Reilly, *Where 20 or 30 are Gathered: Leading Worship in the Small Church*, (Herndon, Virginia: Alban Institute).

2006   Barbara Day Miller, *The New Pastor's Guide to Leading Worship*, (Nashville: Abingdon Press).

2006   James Jordan, *The Musician's Walk: An Ethical Labyrinth*. (Chicago: GIA Publications, Inc).

2005   Norma Dewaal Malefyt, and Howard Vanderwell, *Designing Worship Together: Models and Strategies for Worship Planning (Vital Worship, Healthy Congregations)*, (Herndon, Virginia: Alban Institute).

2002   James Jordan, *The Musician's Spirit*. (Chicago: GIA Publications, Inc).

2001   W. Thomas Smith and Robert J. Batastini, eds. *Hymns for the Gospels*. (Chicago: GIA Publications, Inc).

2001   Paul Westermeyer, *The Heart of the Matter: Church Music as Praise, Prayer, Proclamation, Story, and Gift*. (Chicago: GIA Publications, Inc).

2000   John L. Bell, *The Singing Thing: A Case for Congregational Song*. (Chicago: GIA Publications, Inc).

1999   James Jordan, *The Musician's Soul*. (Chicago: GIA Publications, Inc).

1995   Ruth C. Duck, *Finding Words for Worship: A Guide for Leaders* (Louisville: Westminster John Knox Press).

Notes

1. Frederick Hilborn Talbot, *African American Worship: New Eyes for Seeing.* (Lima, OH: Fairway Press, 1998), 135.
2. Erik Routley, *Church Music and Theology* (Philadelphia: Muhlenburg, 1959), 110.
3. Melva Wilson Costen, *African American Christian Worship*, (Nashville: Abingdon Press, 1993), 135-136.
4. William D. Watley, "Theological Linguistics," an address delivered at the 2000 Hampton University Ministers' Conference, Hampton, VA. To my knowledge, this address has not been published.
5. A. W. Tozer. *Tozer on Worship and Entertainment*, compiled by James L. Snyder. (Camp Hill, PA: Christian Publications, 1997), 101-2.
6. The website for The African American Lectionary is www.theafricanamericanlectionary.org.

Chapter

11

African American Heritage Hymnal: A Worship Resource and Practical Anthology—Part 1

In 1987, GIA Publications made its first effort to publish for the African American church community through the publication of *Lead Me, Guide Me*, a hymnal intended primarily for African American Catholics. Prompted in part by the success of that edition, the Rev. Dr. Delores Carpenter, pastor of the Michigan Park Christian Church in Washington, DC, speaking on behalf of an informal group of pastors and musicians, approached GIA in 1992 with the idea of creating a similar edition for African American Protestant congregations. GIA's interest was immediate and enthusiastic. Dr. Carpenter, general editor, along with her musical colleague, the Rev. Nolan Williams, Jr., music editor, assembled an outstanding committee of pastors and musicians, and on January 17, 1993, their first meeting was held in Washington, DC. I was invited to join the editorial board in 1998. The hymnal was first released and used at the 2001 Hampton University Ministers' and Musicians' Conference, June 4–8, in Hampton, Virginia.

As seventeenth-century enslaved Africans heard sermons and testimonies of God's goodness, love, grace, and mercy, they created songs

African American Heritage Hymnal: A Worship Resource and Practical Anthology—Part 1
Originally published in *GIA Quarterly: A Liturgical Music Journal* 13, no. 4 (2002): 18–21. All rights reserved.

Figure 11.1

I Love the Lord, He Heard My Cry

Figure 11.1, continued

live a - when uh-troub -

le rise, I'll has - ten to His throne,

I a - has -

ten to His, His throne.

Text: African American traditional
Tune: Meter hymn, anonymous; lined out by M. Adams and Louis Sykes
©2000, GIA Publications, Inc.

in response to them. Those they did not create, they adapted and adopted in their own unique style, fashion, and liking. Where the rhythm was straight, they syncopated it. Where they found the meter consistent, they made it inconsistent. If the tempo was too fast, they slowed it down. If the tempo was too slow, they took it faster. If the melody was too simple, they ornamented and embellished it. In essence, they made the songs their own. Dr. Wendell P. Whalum once said, "The Black Methodist and Baptist endorsed [Isaac] Watts's hymns, but the Baptist 'blackened' them. They virtually threw out the meter signature and rhythm and before 1875 had begun a new system which, though based on the style of singing coming from England to America in the eighteenth century, was drastically different from it" ("Black Hymnody" in *Readings in African American Church Music and Worship,* ed. James Abbington [Chicago: GIA Publications, 2001], 174).

This rich and diverse heritage and legacy of the African American religious experience includes the religious folk songs known as "spirituals." These songs, not created by a single individual, but by a group and religious

Figure 11.2

Before This Time Another Year

Figure 11.2, continued

Text: Anonymous
Tune: Meter hymn, anonymous; arr. by M. Adams and Louis Sykes
©2000, GIA Publications, Inc.

community, are captured today in the four-part settings most associated with Euro-American hymnody.

As God continued to be revealed to people of African ancestry in America, the response musically has been opulent and diverse with spirituals, White Protestant psalms, hymns, and spiritual songs, especially those of Isaac Watts and the Wesley brothers, Euro-American anthems, traditional and contemporary gospels, as well as praise and worship songs.

The *African American Heritage Hymnal* is a much-needed and long-awaited worship resource and practical anthology of the rich musical diversity of the African American church. Examples of this diversity can be found throughout the hymnal and are worthy of careful and critical examination. It is the most inclusive compilation of musical and liturgical significance for African American Protestant churches in decades.

Examples of spirituals, or religious folk songs written in four-part harmony, can be found in the arrangements of "Calvary" (239), "Come and Go with Me" (596), "Deep River" (605), "Guide My Feet" (131), "I

109

Figure 11.3

Oh, What He's Done For Me

2. He took my feet out the miry clay, that's...
3. He feeds me when I'm hungry, that's...
4. He picked me up and turned me around, that's...
5. He gave me a home in glory, that's...

Text: Anonymous
Tune: Meter hymn, anonymous; arr. by M. Adams and Louis Sykes
©2000, GIA Publications, Inc.

Know the Lord Has Laid His Hands on Me" (360), "I Wanna Be Ready" (600), "I've Been 'Buked" (386), "New Born Again" (362), "Old Time Religion" (161), "Over My Head" (169), "Plenty Good Room" (352), "This Little Light of Mine" (549), and "Were You There?" (254).

Songs from various African religious traditions are represented in the settings of "Amen Siakudumisa" (122), "Halleluya! Pelo Tsa Rona" (180), "Imela" (535), "Jesu Tawa Pano/Jesus, We Are Here" (401), "Mayenziwe/ Your Will Be Done" (666), "Siyahamba" (164), and "Thuma Mina" (564).

The hymnal contains many of the standard Euro-American Protestant hymns such as "A Mighty Fortress Is Our God" (124), "All Creatures of Our God and King" (147), "All Glory, Laud, and Honor" (226), "Be Still, My Soul" (135), "Brightest and Best" (219), "Crown Him with Many Crowns" (288), "Eternal Father, Strong to Save" (610), "For All the Saints" (339), "Hail to the Lord's Anointed" (187), "Jesus Shall Reign" (289), "Lead On, O King Eternal" (477), "Lift High the Cross" (242), "Love Divine, All Love Excelling" (440), "O Sacred Head Surrounded" (251), "O Thou, in Whose Presence" (422), "Praise to the Lord, the Almighty" (117), "Renew Thy Church, Her Ministries Restore" (343), "Wash, O God, Our Sons and Daughters" (674), and "When, in Our Music, God Is Glorified" (112).

One of the unique qualities of the hymnal is the attempt to notate the tradition of lining meter hymns such as "A Charge to Keep I Have" (467), "Am I a Soldier of the Cross" (483), "Amazing Grace" (272), "Before This Time Another Year" (597), "Guide Me, O Thou Great Jehovah" (139), and "I Love the Lord, He Heard My Cry" (394). The indications *Leader* and *All* in "I Love the Lord, He Heard My Cry" (see Figure 11.1) and "Before This Time Another Year" (see Figure 11.2) are given to illustrate the performance practice of the "leader's" musical call, or the deacon's lining of the texts, and "all," or the congregation's musical response. This tradition is somewhat similar to what is heard in the performance practices of early Gregorian chant. The key to a more authentic performance of these hymns are indicated in the markings *freely,* (467) *slow, very free (ad-lib)* and *gliss.* (394), *slow and freely* (597), the fermatas, grand pauses, and the observance of the breath markings. Moaning of the same musical material is very common in an actual performance of these hymns. Lining hymns has almost become a lost art in most of today's African American churches, although it remains alive and well in churches where the "seasoned" members of the congregation still remember the hymns and sing them as a part of devotional services and prayer meetings, thereby preserving them through oral tradition.

Another unique feature of the *African American Heritage Hymnal* is the notation of early "prayer and praise songs" of the African American church such as "Bless That Wonderful Name of Jesus (295), "Glory, Glory, Hallelujah" (500), "I've Got a Feelin'" (313), "If You Live Right" (582), "Oh, What He's Done for Me" (154) (see Figure 11.3), "So Glad I'm Here" (304, 305), "Satan, We're Gonna Tear Your Kingdom Down" (485) (see Figure 11.4), "The Windows of Heaven" (234), "Until I Found the Lord" (454), and "What a Mighty God We Serve" (478). One must bear in mind that during the performance of these songs, verses tend to be repeated a number of times and new verses added as the Spirit and/ or leader leads. In addition to improvised accompaniments on keyboard instruments, hand clapping, foot patting, tambourine and drum playing are indigenous and characteristic of the performance practice.

"What you see is not always what you get" in the performance of many hymns in the African American church, where rhythms and meters are freely altered and improvised. One excellent example of this can be seen in the hymn "Down at the Cross" (248) (see Figure 11.5), where the rhythms have been carefully notated as they are traditionally sung in most churches. Notice the syncopation between beats 2 and 3 in the first six measures of "Down at the Cross." Another example of this type of alteration is found in "Leaning on the Everlasting Arms" (371). The song is presented here in 12/8 as opposed to the original 4/4 to give a solid triplet feeling on each beat, which is most often performed. The cue notes at the end of measures 4, 8, and 12 give the keyboard player a more stylistic accompaniment heard in a typical rendering of this hymn.

Figure 11.4

Satan, We're Gonna Tear Your Kingdom Down

Text: Traditional
Tune: KINGDOM DOWN, 10 10 12 10; traditional; arr. by Jimmie Abbington, © 2000, GIA Publications, Inc.

Figure 11.5

Down at the Cross

Figure 11.5, continued

Text: Elisha A. Hoffman, 1839–19296
Tune: GLORY TO HIS NAME, 999 7 with refrain; John H. Stockton, 1813–1877;
arr. by Evelyn Simpson-Curenton, b. 1953. © 2000, GIA Publications, Inc.

Chapter

12

African American Heritage Hymnal: A Worship Resource and Practical Anthology—Part 2

Particularly important to this hymnal is the large representation of hymns by African Americans. Reverend Charles A. Tindley (1851–1933), known as the father of African American hymnody and progenitor of African American gospel music, is well represented. In addition to the more familiar hymns "Nothing Between" (397), "We'll Understand It Better By and By" (418), "Leave It There" (420), and "I'll Overcome Someday" (544), two lesser-known but lovely hymns, "Heaven's Christmas Tree" (205) (see Figure 12.1) and "In Me" (452), are included as they appeared in the original collections *New Songs of Paradise,* which are now out of print. A gospel version of Tindley's hymn "The Storm Is Passing Over" (427), which uses only the first verse of the hymn, was arranged by the late gospel recording artist Donald Vails and now appears in print for the first time.

In addition to the pioneering African American gospel hymn writers—Lucie E. Campbell, Doris Akers, Thomas A. Dorsey, Roberta Martin, Kenneth Morris, and others—many of today's African American gospel hymn writers are also included, such as Andrae Crouch, Margaret

African American Heritage Hymnal: A Worship Resource and Practical Anthology—Part 2
Originally published in *GIA Quarterly: A Liturgical Music Journal* 14, no. 1 (2002): 16–19. All rights reserved.

Figure 12.1

Heaven's Christmas Tree

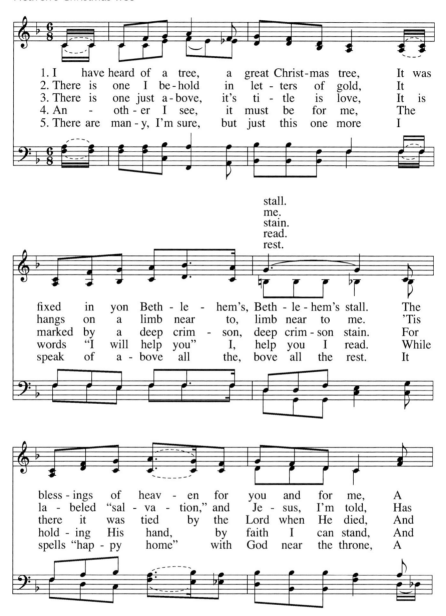

1. I have heard of a tree, a great Christ-mas tree, It was
2. There is one I be-hold in let-ters of gold, It
3. There is one just a-bove, it's ti-tle is love, It is
4. An-oth-er I see, it must be for me, The
5. There are man-y, I'm sure, but just this one more I

stall.
me.
stain.
read.
rest.

fixed in yon Beth-le-hem's, Beth-le-hem's stall. The
hangs on a limb near to, limb near to me. 'Tis
marked by a deep crim-son, deep crim-son stain. For
words "I will help you" I, help you I read. While
speak of a-bove all the, bove all the rest. It

bless-ings of heav-en for you and for me, A
la-beled "sal-va-tion," and Je-sus, I'm told, Has
there it was tied by the Lord when He died, And
hold-ing His hand, by faith I can stand, And
spells "hap-py home" with God near the throne, A

Figure 12.1, continued

Christ - mas pres - ent for all.
bought that pack - age for me.
glo - ry to His dear name.
this is the pack - age I need.
place where the wea - ry shall rest.

There is a pack-age for me on that tree; A pre - cious

to - ken that some-one loves me. Oh yes, I can see on

Cal - va - ry's Tree, That there is a pack-age for me.

Text: Charles A. Tindley
Tune: HEAVEN'S CHRISTMAS TREE, 11 9 11 7 with refrain; Charles A. Tindley; arr. Charles A. Tindley, Jr.

119

Figure 12.2

All My Help Comes from the Lord

Figure 12.2, continued

Text and Tune: Rev. Cleophus Robinson, © 1964, Lion Publishing Co.
Arranged: Evelyn Simpson-Curenton, © 2000, GIA Publications, Inc.

Douroux, V. Michael McKay, Richard Smallwood, Nolan Williams, and Kenneth Louis, to name a few. A complete listing can be found in the Index of Composers, Authors, and Sources (694).

Space will not permit me to discuss in detail all of the unique qualities and inclusions of the *African American Heritage Hymnal,* but one must certainly be aware of some of what I consider to be "sacred jewels" in the collection, such as the traditional gospel settings of "All My Help Comes from the Lord" (370) (see Figure 12.2), "All Night, All Day" (130), "God Never Fails" (159), "He Calmed the Ocean" (223), "I Thank You, Jesus" (532), "I'll Tell It Wherever I Go" (514), "My Soul Loves Jesus" (581), "Peace! Be Still!" (221), "Precious Memories" (516), "Touch Me, Lord Jesus" (274), "There's a Bright Side Somewhere" (411), and "Walking Up the King's Highway" (402).

Well balanced are contemporary gospel and praise-and-worship songs such as "Anointing" (318), "Cast Your Cares" (141), "Center of My Joy" (491), "Come Let Us Praise the Lord" (106), "Hallelujah, Amen" (118), "I Feel Jesus in This Place" (311) "I Really Love the Lord" (577), "I Will Bless Thee, O Lord" (530), "Koinonia" (579) (see Figure 12.3), "Order My Steps" (333), "Perfect Praise" (296), "Praise Him" (172), "Sanctuary" (462), "The Lamb" (179), "The Reason Why I Sing" (496), "Total Praise" (113), "We Won't Leave Here Like We Came" (407), "We Bring the Sacrifice of Praise" (529), and "Welcome to My Father's House" (340).

Worthy of serious consideration are Nolan Williams's "Messiah Now Has Come" (203) (see Figure 12.4), a refreshing addition to Christmas hymnody; "Here Am I" (466); the hauntingly beautiful setting of "O Holy Savior" (408); Evelyn Simpson-Curenton's arrangement of "Close to Thee" (552); and Betty McCullough's "He Will Keep You in Perfect Peace." (495). These compositions certainly add to the immense variety of styles that make the hymnal so universal, ecumenical, desirable, and usable by non-African American churches as well.

The rich and wide musical diversity of the African American worship experience is well documented in the *African American Heritage Hymnal.* It is not only a hymnal to be used in worship services; it is also a tremendous anthology of four centuries of singing and praising God. It reflects the theology that has shaped our music, and the music that has shaped our theology. The herculean task of notating many of the spirituals, traditional gospels, and hymns as they are sung in the African American church has been accomplished by a committee of competent, skilled, and committed musicians who are all actively involved in music ministry in their respective churches and religious communities. Three excellent examples of such work can be seen in Nolan Williams's arrangement of Richard Smallwood's "I Love the Lord, He Heard My Cry" (395) (see Figure 12.5), Joseph Joubert's arrangement of "Precious Memories" (516) (see Figure 12.6), and Stephen Key's arrangement of "Hold to God's Unchanging Hand" (404).

The *African American Heritage Hymnal* is an unparalleled worship resource and a practical anthology that will serve the African American church, musicians, pastors, theologians, historians, hymnologists, and musicologists for many years to come.

Editor's Note: The *African American Heritage Hymnal* was formally received into the permanent collection of the Library of Congress on September 10, 2002, recognized for its historical value as an anthology of African American hymnology and sacred song.

Koinonia   Figure12.3

How   can   I   say   that I   love   the   Lord   whom I've
get   to   say   that I   love   the   one   whom   I

nev -   er,   ev   -   er   seen   be - fore;   and   for -
walk   be - side   each and

1.

2.

ev -   'ry day?   How   can   I   look   up -

on   your   face   and   ig - nore   God's   love?   You   I

Figure 12.3, continued

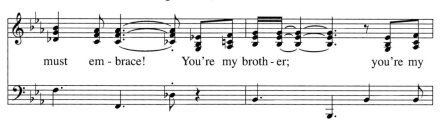

must em-brace! You're my broth-er; you're my

sis-ter; and I love you with the love of my

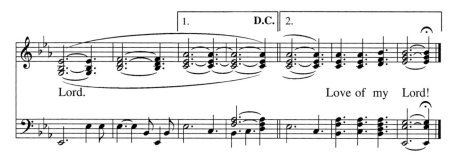

Lord. Love of my Lord!

Text: V. Michael McKay
Tune: V. Michael McKay
© Schaff Music Publishing

Figure 12.4

Messiah Now Has Come

Figure 12.4, continued

God's a-noint-ed One! Now-ell, Now-ell, glad

tid-ings tell, Mes - si-ah now has come!

Text: Nolan Williams, Jr.
Tune: MESSIAH, 54 6 D with refrain; Nolan William, Jr.
© 1996, NEWorks Publishing

Figure 12.5

I Love the Lord, He Heard My Cry

Figure 12.5, continued

live,   while troub-les rise,   I'll has-ten   to

His throne.   I love the

Figure 12.5, continued

throne. I'll has - ten to His throne.

Text and tune: Richard Smallwood, © 1990, Century Oak/Richwood Music
Arranged: Nolan Williams, Jr. © 2000, GIA Publications, Inc.

Figure 12.6

Precious Memories

Figure 12.6, continued

In the still - ness
Je - sus whis - pers,
As I pon - der
In the si - lence

of the mid - night
"I'll be with you."
oh, sweet won - der!
of the mid - night

Sa - cred se - crets He'll un -
What a com - fort to my
Pre - cious mem - 'ries flood my
Pre - cious mem - 'ries flood my

Last time

fold.
soul.
soul.
soul.

Last time

Chapter

13

Waiting to Go! and *Going to Wait!*— Introductions and A Word about the Musical Selections

Waiting to Go!—Introduction

Nikki Giovanni wrote a poem that says, "All I ever do is sit and wait!" Waiting is familiar to people of color. We waited in slave castles for those ships, which would set sail with us as the precious cargo. We waited for the passage of those same ships across dangerous waters. We waited as hunger, humiliation, and even death stalked the hulls where we were stored. We were forced to wait upon auction blocks to be sold as animals. We waited for emancipation as we labored to make ourselves at home in a foreign land. And, we waited for freedom. We continue to wait. Nikki's words are so true and appropriate... "All I ever do is sit and wait!"

Although waiting is not one of our favorite things to do, we have grown accustomed to waiting. Our national dislike of waiting has brought about drive-through lines, ATM machines, e-mail and instant messages, and every

Waiting to Go! and *Going to Wait!*—Introductions and A Word about the Musical Selections
Originally published in a slightly different form in *Waiting to Go!: African American Church Worship Resources from Advent through Pentecost*, James Abbington and Linda H. Hollies (Chicago: GIA Publications, Inc., 2002), 3–4, 7–8 and *Going to Wait!: African American Church Worship Resources between Pentecost and Advent*, James Abbington and Linda H. Hollies (Chicago: GIA Publications, Inc., 2003), 3–4, 8–10. All rights reserved.

type of quick-fix food and even "get-rich-quick" scams! Yet, God requires that we continue to wait. Certain things will not hurry. Certain seasons will not be rushed. Certain journeys require the long way. There are no short cuts. So, God forces us to wait. For waiting is part of God's master plan for life.

The mystery of Advent is that we are forced to wait. Advent signals days of preparing for the birth of the Christ. From the first or second Sunday after Thanksgiving until Christmas Eve, the Christian world is on watch, so we wait on the arrival of the Holy One. Many traditions honor this waiting time by lighting an Advent Candle Wreath. The wait is on. For the next four weeks, we sit. We wait. The Christ is coming. His mother, Mary, is pregnant! We should be pregnant, too!

The candles are purple or blue sometimes a rose colored one is lit on the third Sunday to signal our joy that the day is drawing near. They are lit to indicate that the regal one of glory will soon be arriving. It's not until Christmas Day that we light the huge center candle, which is white and called the Christ Candle. If there is a Christmas Eve worship, it is not appropriate to light that candle until after midnight. We cannot hurry the birth of Jesus Christ. It was both a natural and supernatural event that took time. All the world could do was sit and wait. A pregnancy requires nine months of waiting. Our time is a short wait.

Advent is about waiting, watching, anticipating, expecting, looking forward to and preparing our hearts to be clean mangers for the coming birth. Far too many are continuing to say, like the Innkeeper, "No room." In our congregations, there are too many who want the Child to come to a "room" not clean enough to house him! Therefore, Advent is our time to get ready. For like Mary, we ought be pregnant and ready to give birth to new ways in which to spread the message of Jesus Christ in our world.

The ancient text of the Evangelist Luke calls us to, "Prepare the way for the Lord, make straight paths for him," (Luke 3:4). This says that we are not ready! But, we must get ready. Thank God for waiting time. Thank God that Christ is not about to crack the sky, sound the trumpet, and find too many of us left behind! We want to run head-long, quick, fast, and in a hurry to get to the festive season of Christmas. However, since it did take Jesus forty-two generations to get to us in human form, surely we can prepare for four weeks to celebrate his birth.

Yes! We are forced to wait. And in our waiting, we consider our ways. In our waiting, we repent of our sin. In our waiting, we re-connect with our community. In our waiting, we make room in our busy lives for others. In our waiting, we prepare to receive the Host of Heaven who comes to tabernacle to feed us with the Bread of Heaven, which satisfies our hungry, waiting souls.

If there is any one nation that knows the importance of waiting, it is the Black Church. Watch Night worships began as groups of us got together to "watch the days of slavery" disappear with the signing of the Emancipation Proclamation document. We were ready to go!

People were not always certain of their new destinations, but they gathered together in preparation to go to a new place, a new freedom, new beginnings. Advent prepares us for the One who was born to die and give us an Easter to celebrate. Advent helps us to walk the Lenten journey to Calvary with Jesus. Then Advent gives us the required spiritual muscles to wait for the arrival of the Holy Spirit at Pentecost! Pentecost is our signal to go! We are to go, at Pentecost, into all the world and tell them about the Savior who came to send us out to reach them in his name!

Waiting to Go! is a resource book, a ready-to-use book, and a workbook designed to help congregational worship leaders and musicians with their ministries. Classical scriptures, held sacred down through the centuries, will be offered as guides to the Christian year. Appropriate music, hymns, gospel, Anthems, traditional, contemporary, and especially that provided by African American artists will be uplifted. Sermon suggestions will assist in tying together the theological themes that arise between Hebrew Scripture, Psalms, and Gospel passages. This book will become an invaluable guide that will complement those traditions that are sacred to your particular congregation. Let the Holy Spirit minister through these suggestions as we each prepare, *Waiting to Go!*

Going to Wait!—Introduction

God is! The blanks can be filled in with so many various and descriptive adjectives. Any one that we use fails to adequately encompass the length, breath and depth of who and what God really is in this world and beyond.

135

Writing this in the fall season, on a color tour through the eastern portion of our nation, I can tell you that God is an artist of indescribable comprehension! Looking at groves of trees nestled upon the Allegheny Mountains, the scene takes away my breath. The sky is azure blue; the clouds are fluffy and white. The fields are golden. The cooling water meanders here and there; streams, rivers, creeks and lakes. But, upon the hills sit a collective of colors painted every color imaginable. God is artist extraordinaire!

Who told which trees to turn a sparkling orange, dazzling red, brilliant yellow, hazy shades of purple or evergreen? Who whispered "change" to the season and sent a nip into the air; falling leaves to the ground; told flowers to fade but chrysanthemums to bud? Who orchestrated the winds to shift; told warm weather to fade and called colder air to be summoned from the north water reservoirs? What producer told fruit, grain and potatoes to yield their crop? What force dispatched little birds to begin their flight south? Who speaks to caterpillars the time to begin their metamorphosis process of spinning cocoons? Who tells earth to shut down production and to prepare for winter rest? What power forces fish to sink lower into undisturbed waters while bears begin to feel and to experience their slumber throughout another season? As the leaves fall, not one looks like another. The snowflakes are being prepared, one by one, each one already accounted for and named! What makes these mountains stand, yielding coal generation after generation, warming a world that knew nothing of fire when Adam and Eve were created? How is it that clouds above keep oceans and rivers afloat, and trees provide both air and protection from the sun?

All of Mother Nature's magnificence calls forth our hymns of praise and worship. "Great Is Thy Faithfulness" surely testifies to God's artistry without painter, landscape artist or production crew! "Our God Is an Awesome God," merely whispers at the awesomeness of the Creator.

For no one word can ever contain our adoration of God. There is not any single human element of speech to provide expression of all God is! Therefore, we simply worship God in singing hymns. Hymns magnify God. Hymns declare our worship of the Ancient of Days. Hymns address our need to say something about our adoration of the One Who Was, the One Who Is and the One Who Is To Come! Hymns concentrate our attention on the First and the Last. Hymns utter our unspeakable thanks to the Giver of All!

A hymn takes our focus from us. A hymn's focus is the Great I Am, who, though available to us, is far beyond us, even above and beneath us. A hymn removes our train of thought from our immediate condition, circumstances and situations to point us toward our help, our protection, our refuge and our shelter. A hymn moves us to look up! A hymn pulls us to magnify the Sovereign God who is yet in control of the whole wide world. All is well with a hymn for our God reigns!

Hymns call us to true worship. Hymns help us to see God's vast glory. Hymns help us to remember what God has already done. We join with the angelic forces to bow down in reverence before God's throne as we worship with a hymn. Hymns assist us in believing that what God has done already, down through the ages, God will "encore!" God will do it again, in our time, the hymns assure us as they anchor our faith in the Mystery.

The God of every season is faithful. The God of winter's frozen, sleeping beauty does it again, year after year. That's faithfulness. The God of overcast days and cloudy skies is the same God who speaks buds into sprouting and glaciers begin to float in the spring. That's faithfulness. The God of warming air is the same God who commands the sun to become butter yellow and the birds to migrate back to sing for us again in the summer heat. That's faithfulness. And, it's this same God who prepares an abundant harvest for the world's nourishment in the fall. That's faithfulness. Hymns attempt to capture God's faithful wonders and set them to music for us to express our thanks and appreciation.

As the Church "goes into all the world" we need marching music. We need the melody that ties us with the faithful who went before us. Our children, grandchildren and great-grandchildren, for as many generations as the Lord allows to follow us, need to know the tunes of our faith in God. So, we place special emphasis on hymns and anthems in *Waiting to Go!* and *Going to Wait!*

Kirk Franklin, Yolanda Adams, Mary and John P. Kee utilize the messages of ancient tunes! They have updated the tempo, contemporized the melody and added new beats, but they continue to depend upon the sacred words of the Church's great hymns and anthems. These "new artists" are not original. For the deeds, acts, movements, miracles and signs of God have been noted and penned down through the years. Ecclesiastes 1:9 reminds us, "There is nothing new under the sun."

There is a difference between hymns, anthems, gospel and contemporary music. We need to teach our young people the full range of our faith. It's wonderful to have the "boomers" coming back to the Church. It's awesome to have our youth "fishing for religion." Plus, we only exist due to the thrill of having our elders remain in our pews as anchors to our past. Each one of these groups needs to be musically fed and challenged to grow in our faith journey. Teaching, singing and utilizing the hymns and anthems allow for inter-generational worship. Watch the faces of the congregation as a soloist sings a metered hymn and then the Praise Team or choir swings into the rhythm that is popular today. We are all on the journey together! This army needs to march to a coordinated beat. Let's keep singing till the power of the Lord comes down to dwell among us, tabernacle within us, and remain within us as we Go to Wait!

A Word about the Musical Selections*

Martin Luther once said that music is a gift of God "instilled and implanted in all creatures...from the beginning of the world. Nothing is without sound or harmony, but the human voice is the most wonderful gift of all. Therefore, next to the Word of God, music deserves the highest praise."

It is in that spirit that I have had the distinct privilege of entering into a harmonious partnership with Reverend Dr. Linda H. Hollies to make this project possible. Dr. Hollies has provided the Scripture lessons, focus, prayers, and visual arts suggestions for each Sunday from Advent through Pentecost. My task has been to provide musical suggestions that will complement, enhance, reinforce, and support the texts and focus of the day.

While my musical suggestions are not intended to be the complete, final, or definitive selections, they are offered to provide a general direction and focus for planning music for the worship service for the various Sundays. The possibilities are endless! Composers are always writing new compositions, and previously written compositions are being uncovered and reprinted.

Because no particular hymnal in the African American church could provide all of the variety and diversity needed for the scope of this project, I have selected the following hymnals for consideration along with their abbreviations throughout this book:

* The information in this section is a merging of the material found in the separate volumes.

AAHH *African American Heritage Hymnal* (Chicago: GIA Publications, 2001)

AME *AMEC Bicentennial Hymnal* (Nashville: The African Methodist Episcopal Church, 1984)

AMEZ *The African Methodist Episcopal Zion Bicentennial Hymnal* (New York: The African Methodist Episcopal Zion Church, 1996)

LEVS *Lift Every Voice and Sing II: An African American Hymnal* (New York: The Church Hymnal Corporation, 1993)

LMGM *Lead Me, Guide Me: The African American Catholic Hymnal* (Chicago: GIA Publications, 1987)

NNBH *The New National Baptist Hymnal—21st Century Edition* (Nashville: Triad Publications, 1987).*

TFBF *This Far by Faith* (Minneapolis: Augsburg Fortress, 1999).*

YL *Yes, Lord! Church of God in Christ Hymnal* (Memphis: The Church of God in Christ Publishing Board, 1982)

HG *Hymns for the Gospels* (Chicago: GIA Publications, 2001)

Other resources for spirituals and organ music that I frequently recommend include the following:

The Oxford Book of Spirituals. Edited by Moses Hogan (New York: Oxford University Press, 2002).
The Anthology of African American Organ Music, Volumes 1–4. Edited by Dr. Mickey Thomas Terry (St. Louis, MO: MorningStar Music Publishers) [ongoing].
Songs of Deliverance: Organ Arrangements and Congregational Acts of Worship for the Church Year Based on African American Spirituals. By William Farley Smith (Nashville: Abingdon Press, 1996).

---

* The New National Baptist Hymnal—21st Century Edition *and* This Far by Faith *are referenced in* Going to Wait! *only.*

139

After considering the Scripture lessons and focus for the Sunday, specific themes, emphases, and key words emerged that guided my selection of appropriate hymns, anthems, spirituals, and gospel selections, as well as organ music. I am certainly aware of the various levels of ability and competency among church music personnel and the variety of instruments that exist in African American churches, and have offered a variety of selections that I hope will provide direction for your thinking and selection process.

Noticeably absent from the listings are suggestions for children's choirs, handbells, instrumental ensembles, and praise and worship teams. It is my hope that titles listed will provide adequate ideas and insight for making those selections. I do not claim to be a specialist in those areas, and therefore make no attempt to offer suggestions. However, a project that includes those selections is much needed.

Pastors, music directors, musicians, and worship leaders should invest in a variety of hymnals for their library for a broader use and selection of hymnody for the congregation. The Hymn Society in the United States and Canada provides the most current and reliable resources for church music. I strongly recommend membership in that organization. The toll-free number is 1(800) THE HYMN.

While the accessibility of musical resources written by African Americans has been rather limited in the past, there are more musical selections available now than ever. Most of today's current gospel music by recording artists is available in sheet music and can be ordered from local music dealers. I have personally experienced a tremendous amount of cooperation and success with "N" Time Music in Charlotte, NC. They offer gospel sheet music, songbooks, cassettes and CDs, performance soundtracks and much more. Their address is 4913 Albemarle Road, Charlotte, NC 28205. Their email address is info@ntimemusic.com, and the website is www.ntimemusic.com.

I have also enjoyed many years of reliable, dependable, and courteous service with Lois Fyfe Music in Nashville, TN for all of my choral music and organ music needs. Their address is 2209 Crestmoor Road, Suite 220, Nashville, TN 37215. They can also be reached by calling toll-free 1(800) 851-9023. Every choir director and musician should establish a consistent and amicable relationship with a music dealer, which brings me to a very critical issue.

I am most obligated to share with the reader that it is illegal to photocopy music! Composers of great music can not and will not benefit from our illegal photocopying and reproduction of their music. The rewards for their work that we so enjoy are never experienced as long as good, God-fearing church choir directors and musicians keep running to the photocopier and illegally reproducing their music. There are very stringent laws that protect these composers, and it is the responsibility of the church leaders to ensure that those laws are not violated. Please be very mindful of this as you select and perform music.

I am indebted to my friend and colleague, Tony McNeill, Director of Music Ministries at the Friendship Missionary Baptist Church in Charlotte, NC, for allowing me to include his research in the Appendix, which contains descriptions of extended sacred works by contemporary African American composers. The Selected Bibliography is intended to recommend additional resources that will provide assistance in planning music for worship.

In the Appendix of Resources, I have included the titles of arrangements compiled in *WOW Gospel Songbook Collection,* an annual publication by various gospel artists from 1998 through 2003. I encourage you to peruse the lists as you plan and select music for your worship services and choirs. Again, "N" Time Music in Charlotte, NC is an excellent source of all of these and many more gospel music compositions.

In his classic book, *Church Music and Theology*, Erik Routley said, "When the minister and musician refuse to communicate with one another…at worst it will be, as it often in practice is, a wicked waste of an opportunity for glorifying God through fruitful partnership." It is my sincere hope and prayer that *Waiting to Go!* will provide an ongoing opportunity for dialogue and communication between the minister and the musician. This "fruitful partnership," so desperately needed, will provide a wonderful catalyst by which the pulpit and the choir loft can more effectively lead the People of God in worship. This kind of planning and collaboration will certainly elevate and enhance music and worship in the African American church to new and ultimate dimensions that please and honor God!

—James Abbington
and Linda H. Hollies

Chapter

14

New Wine in Old Wineskins— Introduction

In a lecture at the 1995 Hampton University Ministers' Conference, The Reverend Dr. J. Wendell Mapson, Jr., Pastor of the Monumental Baptist Church in Philadelphia, Pennsylvania, passionately declared that:

> The hymns . . . should be sung enthusiastically with the congregation standing. If the hymns are dead, it is because the people who sing them are dead . . . Congregational hymn singing is almost a lost art in the Black church. We allow the choir to do all the singing with their special arrangements and contemporary songs that people may enjoy, but cannot participate[.]

> This spectator worship is not the kind of worship pleasing to God. Congregational singing is in the intensive care unit breathing its last breath. Let's go back to the hymnal and resurrect those hymns of our faith, and sing them with life, and spirit, and joy . . . [1]

Of all the musical instruments that may be employed in the praise of God, the human voice has priority. Other instruments are to be used primarily

New Wine in Old Wineskins—Introduction
Originally published in *New Wine in Old Wineskins: A Contemporary Congregational Song Supplement, Volume 1*, ed. James Abbington (Chicago: GIA Publications, Inc., 2007), 11–15. All rights reserved.

in the service of the singing of God's people. Reformed theologian Karl Barth points out that singing is not an option for the people of God; it is one of the essential ministries of the church:

> The Christian church sings. It is not a choral society. Its singing is not a concert. But from inner, material necessity it sings. Singing is the highest form of human expression . . . What we can and must say quite confidently is that the church which does not sing is not the church. And where . . . it does not really sing but sighs and mumbles spasmodically, shamefacedly and with an ill grace, it can be at best only a troubled community which is not sure of its cause and of whose ministry and witness there can be no great expectation . . . The praise of God which finds its concrete culmination in the singing of the community is one of the indispensable forms of the ministry of the church.[2]

"Congregational singing is a well-known device for the temporary reduction of social alienation and for the accomplishment of an ad interim sense of community" wrote C. Eric Lincoln and Lawrence Mamiya. "In the Black church, singing together is not so much an effort to find, or to establish, a transitory community as it is the reaffirmation of a common bond that, while inviolate, has suffered the pain of separation since the last occasion of physical togetherness."[3]

Congregational singing is to be a purposeful act in worship, never merely a time-filler or a matter of routine. "By means of corporate voiced songs, a call to worship can be sounded, praise can be declared, faith can be confessed, a text from the Bible can be heralded, repentance can be invited, a prayer can be offered, and sacrifice can be encouraged," says S. Paul Schilling in his classic *The Faith We Sing*. Over an extended period of time, the church's worship is strengthened if congregational singing is utilized in service to all of these purposes.

Congregations should sing the fullness of Scripture and the times. Hymns provide the community an opportunity to express its beliefs about faith, doctrine, and the experiences of the Christian life. To be an authentic expression of faith, the beliefs embodied in the hymns must be true, based on Scripture, in keeping with the accepted doctrines of the congregation, and relevant to the people that sing them. Hymns should contribute to our spiritual formation, expressing doctrinal truths about God the Father and God's presence in the world; truths about Jesus Christ the Son and His work as Savior and Redeemer; and truths about the Holy Spirit, the Enabler and Comforter. These are the theological expressions. Theology, the study and understanding of God, is a significant part of hymnology, the study and understanding of hymns. This understanding is essential for the pastor, worship leader, and musicians who must lead the people of God in worship.

I have been extraordinarily privileged over the years to establish relationships and associations with such distinguished organizations and institutions as The Hymn Society in the United States and Canada, The Calvin Institute of Christian Worship at Calvin College in Grand Rapids, Michigan, GIA Publications in Chicago, Illinois, and others. Likewise, I have been fortunate to meet and nurture friendships with illustrious, established, renowned, and prominent hymn writers such as Carl P. Daw, Jr., Ruth Duck, Herman G. Stuempfle, Jr., Mary Louise Bringle, Brian Wren, John Bell, and others. Through these associations I have been introduced to the texts of Shirley Erena Murray, Sylvia Dunstan, Martin E. Leckebusch, Jane Parker Huber, Fred Kaan, and many others.

What I began to discover from my experiences in the African American churches I was privileged to serve was that these profound, prophetic, beautiful, and relevant texts were not being sung, and indeed were not even known. This situation is not unique to African American churches, but is symptomatic of all worshipping communities who are either addicted to the same hymns and unwilling to learn anything new, or simply unaware of texts written since the publication of their denominational hymnal. The majority of these texts have been written in the last twenty or twenty-five years and are not known in many mainline churches. Surveys of hymnody in congregations repeatedly indicate that, while new hymnals and supplements are continually being published, for the most part we sing the same old and familiar hymns. This is problematic in that it causes us to limit our ability to grow biblically, theologically, and liturgically.

When I presented my proposal for this compilation to GIA Publications, they were enthusiastic and very supportive of my vision and desire to expand, enhance, and enrich the hymnody in our churches. I did not want this to be an exclusively African American resource, but, rather, a collection of the very best of congregational song for all of the people of God.

The title *New Wine in Old Wineskins* is a twist on the original passages from the Synoptic Gospels (Matt 9:17, Mark 2:22, Luke 5:37–38). I immediately anticipated the criticism of biblical scholars and New Testament devotees when I selected the title. While in the Gospels Jesus clearly says that no one puts new wine into old wineskins, I chose to borrow that concept as a metaphor for this collection in which the "new wine" represents contemporary hymn texts written by some of today's finest hymn writers, and the "old wineskins" represent tried and true hymn tunes to which these texts have been set for immediate accessibility.

When considering the relationship between a particular text and tune, we can ask if it fits any of the following categories listed by Brian Wren in his unparalleled book *Praying Twice: The Music and Words of Congregational Song*. Some of Wren's categories can be investigated by singing different common meter, long meter, or short meter tunes to the same texts, using the metrical index of a hymnal.

- *Disconnection*: Text and tune are strangers or nodding acquaintances. Neither has much impact on the other.

- *Opposition*: Text and tune are at odds with each other. The most frequent North American choice for Edmund Sears's hymn "It Came upon the Midnight Clear" is CAROL, a lullaby waltz that contradicts the lyric's original (and often eviscerated) protest against war and poverty.

- *Compatibility*: Text and tune are hospitable to each other. Some tunes are "open" to a variety of lyrics. When searching for a public-domain tune to pair with a new lyric, I often find sixteenth-, seventeenth-, and eighteenth-century tunes more accommodating than their nineteenth-century successors . . .

- *Lift off*: A pleasing tune "carries" an undistinguished, undesirable, or archaic lyric . . .

- *Unity*: When music is well matched to its text, "the music dramatizes, explains, underlines, 'breathes life' into the words, resulting in more meaning than the words themselves could express" and a more powerful effect than text or music alone[4] ...Pairings like "Our God, Our Help in Ages Past" / ST. ANNE; "Amazing Grace" / AMAZING GRACE (NEW BRITAIN); and "Hark! the Herald Angels Sing" / MENDELSSOHN are nowadays widely experienced as "natural" or "inevitable."[5]

These were guiding principles throughout the selection and editing process for *New Wine in Old Wineskins*.

Unique to this collection are hymns, gospel songs, and contemporary music for congregational singing by such pioneering African American composers as Harry T. Burleigh, Charles A. Tindley, Charles P. Jones, Gladstone T. Haywood, Dr. Margaret Pleasant Douroux (the reigning queen of African American gospel hymnody), Charles Watkins, C. Eric Lincoln, J. Jefferson Cleveland, Laymon T. Hunter, Eli Wilson, Jr., Jimmy Dowell, and Eddie Robinson. One of these contemporary compositions, by Mr. Robinson, is an example of a community working together to enliven its faith through congregational singing. "We Study, We Shout, We Serve" serves as the mission statement of the New Mt. Olive Baptist Church in Ft. Lauderdale, Florida.

Brian Wren asserts "Congregational song is by nature corporate, corporeal, and inclusive; at its best, it is creedal, ecclesial, inspirational, and evangelical. Each characteristic is theologically important."[6] He continues,

> Whether classical or popular, congregational song . . . should aim to be one or more of the following:
>
> - *Formative*, shaping and modeling our faith as it tells a story within the whole story of God in Christ and draws us into the drama of God's saving love;
>
> - *Transformative*, moving us from isolation to belonging, indifference to interest, interest to conviction, and conviction to commitment;

• *Cognitive*, giving us something to ponder and think about;

• *Educational*, teaching us something we didn't know about the Bible, the church, and Christian faith;

• *Inspirational*, lifting us out of ourselves into hope, joy, and peace.[7]

Special attention was given to including hymns which will help to fill voids in the current repertoire of hymns for the Christian year: there are hymns that address topics such as Advent, Transfiguration, Resurrection Sunday (Easter), and Pentecost. Neglected themes such as forgiveness, healing, reconciliation, unity, justice, and service were addressed, along with the more familiar topics of praise and adoration, worship, thanksgiving, assurance, and comfort. Also included in this collection are two extraordinary hymns by Mary Louise Bringle: "As the Waters Rise around Us," written as a response to the devastation caused by Hurricane Katrina, and "When Terror Streaks through Morning Skies," a succinct appeal for divine help in coping with the events of September 11, 2001.

Wren concludes his herculean work by asserting that "besides giving memorable, liturgical expression to theological themes elaborated more systematically elsewhere, the best hymns act as worthy partners to other theological work by expressing Christian faith in metaphor, epigram, and descriptive images which combine impact with economy, and whose metaphors may sometimes be cognitive, expanding our knowledge in a way inaccessible to reasoned exposition."[8]

Those whose ministry in the church involves music are fond of quoting Ephesians 5:19, "Speak to yourselves in psalms and hymns and spiritual songs . . ." Dietrich Bonhoeffer, one of the most widely read religious writers and theologians of the twentieth century, further expounded, "Our song on earth is speech. It is the sung Word. Why do Christians sing when they are together? The reason is, quite simply, because in singing together it is possible for them to speak and pray the same Word at the same time; in other words, because here they can unite in the Word."[9]

It is my sincere hope that the words and familiar music in this compilation will bless, edify, comfort, challenge, enlighten, illumine, teach, and admonish the people of God. If we are to sing and pray with spirit and understanding, we must mean what we say and sing, and know what we mean. As a seasoned citizen of the church once said, "It ain't no use singing about it if you don't do it." Perhaps more sublimely, S. Paul Schilling said, "Unless the hymns, or congregational songs used in corporate worship, express our real convictions, we might as well sing the stock market reports, the real estate ads from the daily newspaper, or a list of names from the telephone directory."[10]

May this first volume of *New Wine in Old Wineskins* serve the church by providing congregational song that is formative, transformative, cognitive, educational, and inspirational. May all who serve God's people as writers, composers, or leaders of worship and music be stirred by the intoxication of the Spirit to continue creating new hymns and to lead the people of God in new ways of expressing and living their faith.

My eternal gratitude is extended to:

> • The staff of GIA Publications for their support of and work on this volume, especially Alec Harris, President; Robert Batastini, Senior Editor, ret.; Kelly Dobbs Mickus, Senior Editor; Jeff Mickus, Hymnal Coordinator; and Michael Boschert, Editorial Production Assistant; and to Martha Chlipala for the cover art.

> • My brilliant colleague, Michael J. Brown, for the contribution of his introductory essay to this collection.

> • My models of academic excellence for their friendship and encouragement: Don E. Saliers, C. Michael Hawn, Paul Westermeyer, Paul Richardson, John Witvliet, James H. Cone, Joyce Ann Zimmerman, Emily Brink, Barbara Day Miller, Horace C. Boyer, Carlton R. Young, Harry Eskew, and S. T. Kimbrough, Jr.

> • Colleagues, administrators, and students of the Candler School of Theology for their kind support.

> • Marie-Elena Grosett, whose father was Harry T. Burleigh's godson, for the original manuscripts of Mr. Burleigh.

• Daisy Ann Barlow, my mother, for her unfailing love and prayers.

—James Abbington, Editor
Atlanta, 2007

Notes

1. J. Wendell Mapson, Jr., *Strange Fire: A Study of Worship and Liturgy in the African American Church* (St. Louis, MO: Hodale Press, 1996), 85.
2. Karl Barth, *Church Dogmatics*, Vol. IV (London: Continuum Intl. Pub. Group, 2004) part 3, chapter 16, par. 72, #4.
3. C. Eric Lincoln and Lawrence H. Mamiya, *The Black Church in the African American Experience* (Durham, NC: Duke University Press, 1990), 347.
4. Hustad, Donald P., *Jubilate II: Church Music in Worship and Renewal* (Carol Stream, IL: Hope Publishing Company, 1993), 31 and 25–26.
5. Brian Wren, *Praying Twice: The Music and Words of Congregational Song* (Louisville, KY: Westminster John Knox Press, 2000), 77–78.
6. Ibid., 84.
7. Ibid., 71.
8. Ibid., 377.
9. Dietrich Bonhoeffer, *Life Together: The Classic Exploration of Faith Community* (San Francisco: HarperCollins Publishers, 1954), 59.
10. S. Paul Schilling, *The Faith We Sing* (Philadelphia: Westminster Press, 1983), 23.

Acknowledgments

Chapter 1 "There Is a Balm in Gilead": Metamorphosis and Implications for Performance

Originally published in a slightly different form in *The Hymn: A Journal of Congregational Song* 58, no. 2 (2007): 44–48.

Chapter 2 Accompanying Unaccompanied Negro Spirituals: A Musical Oxymoron

Originally published in a slightly different form in *The Hymn: A Journal of Congregational Song* 58, no. 1 (2007): 47–50.

Chapter 3 *Spirits That Dwell in Deep Woods*—Editor's Preface

Originally published in a slightly different form in *Spirits That Dwell in Deep Woods: The Prayer and Praise Hymns of the Black Religious Experience*, Wyatt Tee Walker, ed. James Abbington (Chicago: GIA Publications, Inc., 2003), ix–x.

Chapter 4 Bishop Charles Price Jones (1865–1949)

Originally published in a slightly different form in *The African American Pulpit* 9, no. 1:23–25

Chapter 5 *Beams of Heaven: Hymns of Charles Albert Tindley (1851–1933)*—Introduction

Originally published in *Beams of Heaven: Hymns of Charles Albert Tindley (1851–1933)*, ed. S. T. Kimbrough, Jr., music ed. Carlton R. Young (New York: GBGMusik, 2006), v–xii.

Chapter 6   Suggested Interpretations for Three Gospel Hymns
                   by Margaret Pleasant Douroux

                   Originally published in a slightly different form in *The
                   Hymn: A Journal of Congregational Song* 58, no. 3
                   (2007): 48–51.

Chapter 7   Contemporary Congregational Songs
                   by V. Michael McKay

                   Originally published in a slightly different form in *The
                   Hymn: A Journal of Congregational Song* 58, no. 4
                   (2007): 52–56.

Chapter 8   Pastoral Responsibility in the Music
                   and Worship of the Church

                   Originally published in *The African American Pulpit* 8,
                   no. 3:14–17

Chapter 9   Nonmusical Considerations for the Church Musician

                   Originally published in a slightly different form in *The
                   Musician's Walk: An Ethical Labyrinth*, ed. James Jordan
                   (Chicago: GIA Publications, Inc., 2006), 255–73.

Chapter 10   Worship Resources for Pastors and Musicians

                   Originally published in a slightly different form in
                   The National Baptist Voice, Winter 2005, 46–47

Chapter 11   *African American Heritage Hymnal*: A Worship
                   Resource and Practical Anthology—Part 1

                   Originally published in *GIA Quarterly: A Liturgical
                   Music Journal* 13, no. 4 (2002): 18–21.

Chapter 12   *African American Heritage Hymnal*: A Worship
                   Resource and Practical Anthology—Part 2

                   Originally published in *GIA Quarterly: A Liturgical
                   Music Journal* 14, no. 1 (2002): 16–19.

Chapter 13   *Waiting to Go!* and *Going to Wait!*—Introductions and A Word about the Musical Selections

Originally published in a slightly different form in *Waiting to Go!: African American Church Worship Resources from Advent through Pentecost*, James Abbington and Linda H. Hollies (Chicago: GIA Publications, Inc., 2002), 3–4, 7–8 and *Going to Wait!: African American Church Worship Resources between Pentecost and Advent*, James Abbington and Linda H. Hollies (Chicago: GIA Publications, Inc., 2003), 3–4, 8–10

Chapter 14   *New Wine in Old Wineskins*—Introduction

Originally published in *New Wine in Old Wineskins: A Contemporary Congregational Song Supplement, Volume 1*, ed. James Abbington (Chicago: GIA Publications, Inc., 2007), 11–15.

Bibliography

Abbington, James. *Let Mt. Zion Rejoice! Music in the African American Church.* Valley Forge: Judson, 2001.

————, ed. *Readings in African American Church Music and Worship.* Chicago: GIA, 2001.

Abernethy, Alexis D., ed. *Worship That Changes Lives: Multidisciplinary and Congregational Perspectives on Spiritual Transformation.* Grand Rapids: Baker Academic, 2008.

Aghahowa, Brenda Eatman. *Praising in Black and White: Unity and Diversity in Christian Worship.* Cleveland: United Church, 1996.

Anderson, Leith. *A Church for the 21ˢᵗ Century: Bringing Change to Your Church to Meet the Challenges of a Changing Society.* Minneapolis: Bethany House, 1992.

Baldwin, Lewis V. *To Make the Wounded Whole: The Cultural Legacy of Martin Luther King, Jr.* Minneapolis: Augsburg Fortress, 1992.

Ballou, Hugh. *Moving Spirits, Building Lives: The Church Musician as Transformational Leader.* Kearney, NE: Morris, 2005.

Begbie, Jeremy S. *Resounding Truth: Christian Wisdom in the World of Music.* Grand Rapids: Baker Academic, 2007.

Bell, Derrick. *Gospel Choirs: Psalms of Survival in an Alien Land Called Home.* New York: Basic Books, 1996.

Bell, Jerome. *Bridging the Gap between the Music Department & the Pulpit.* Capital Heights, MD: Xulon, 2006.

Bell, John L. *The Singing Thing: A Case for Congregational Song.* Chicago: GIA, 2000.

Bell, John L. *The Singing Thing Too: Enabling Congregations to Sing.*
Chicago: GIA, 2007.

Berkley, James D., ed. *Leadership Handbook of Preaching and Worship.*
Grand Rapids: Baker Book, 1992.

Best, Harold M. *Music through the Eyes of Faith.* New York:
HarperCollins, 1993.

Black, Kathy. *Culturally-Conscious Worship.* Atlanta: Chalice, 2000.

Blount, Bryant K., ed. *True to Our Native Land: An African American
New Testament Commentary.* Minneapolis: Fortress, 2007.

Borsch, Frederick Houk. *Introducing the Lessons of the Church Year:
A Guide for Lay Readers and Congregations.* New York: Seabury,
1978.

Bower, Peter C., ed. *Handbook for the Revised Common Lectionary.*
Louisville: Westminster John Knox, 1996.

Boyer, Horace Clarence. *How Sweet the Sound: The Golden Age of
Gospel.* Washington, DC: Elliott & Clark, 1995.

Bradley, C. Randall. *From Postlude to Prelude: Music Ministry's Other
Six Days.* Fenton, MO: MorningStar Music, 2004.

Brown, Frank Burch. *Inclusive yet Discerning: Navigating Worship
Artfully.* Grand Rapids: William B. Eerdmans, 2009.

Brueggemann, Walter. *The Message of the Psalms: A Theological
Commentary.* Minneapolis: Augsburg, 1984.

————. *Praying the Psalms: Engaging Scripture and the Life of the
Spirit.* Eugene, OR: Cascade Books, 2007.

————. *The Psalms and the Life of Faith.* Edited by Patrick D. Miller.
Minneapolis: Fortress, 1995.

Burnin, Mellonee V. and Portia K. Maultsby, eds. *African American
Music: An Introduction.* New York: Routledge, 2006.

Burroughs, Bob. *An ABC Primer for Church Musicians.* Nashville:
Broadman, 1990.

Bush, Peter and Christine O'Reilly. *Where 20 or 30 Are Gathered: Leading Worship in the Small Church.* Herndon, VA: Alban Institute, 2006.

Byars, Ronald P. *Future of Protestant Worship: Beyond the Worship Wars*. Louisville: Westminster John Knox, 2002

Carpenter, Bil. *Uncloudy Days: The Gospel Music Encyclopedia.* San Francisco: Backbeat Books, 2005.

Carson, Tim and Kathy. *So You're Thinking about Contemporary Worship.* St. Louis: Chalice, 1997.

Causey, C. Harry. *Things They Didn't Tell Me about Being a Minister of Music.* Rockville, MD: Music Revelation, 1988.

Chapman, Mark L. *Christianity on Trial: African-American Religious Thought Before and After Black Power.* Maryknoll, NY: Orbis Books, 1996.

Chenu, Bruno. *The Trouble I've Seen: The Big Book of Negro Spirituals.* Valley Forge: Judson, 2003.

Cherwien, David M. *Let the People Sing!* St. Louis: Concordia, 1997.

Clark, Linda J. *How We Seek God Together: Exploring Worship Styles.* Herndon, VA: Alban Institute, 2001.

———. *Music in Churches: Nourishing Your Congregation's Musical Life.* Herndon, VA: Alban Institute, 1994.

Cone, James H. *The Spiritual and the Blues.* Maryknoll, NY: Orbis Books, 1972.

Costen, Melva Wilson. *African American Christian Worship*, updated ed. Nashville: Abingdon, 2007.

———. *In Spirit and In Truth: The Music of African American Worship.* Louisville: Westminster John Knox, 2004.

Darden, Robert. *People Get Ready! A New History of Black Gospel Music.* New York: Continuum International, 2006.

Davidson, James Robert. *A Dictionary of Protestant Church Music.* Metuchen, NJ: Scarecrow, 1975.

Davies, J. G., ed. *The New Westminster Dictionary of Liturgy and Worship.* Philadelphia: Westminster, 1986.

Davis, Valerie B. and Safiyah Fosua. *The Africana Worship Book: Year A.* Nashville: Discipleship Resources, 2006.

———. *The Africana Worship Book: Year B.* Nashville: Discipleship Resources, 2007.

———. *The Africana Worship Book: Year C.* Nashville: Discipleship Resources, 2008.

———. *Companion to the Africana Worship Book.* Nashville: Discipleship Resources, 2007.

Dawn, Marva J. *Reaching Out without Dumbing Down: A Theology of Worship for the Turn-of-the-Century Culture.* Grand Rapids: William B. Eerdmans, 1995.

———. *A Royal "Waste" of Time: The Splendor of Worshiping God and Being Church for the World.* Grand Rapids: William B. Eerdmans, 1999.

Dean, Talmage W. *A Survey of Twentieth Century Protestant Church Music in America.* Nashville: Broadman, 1988.

deWaal Malefyt, Norma and Howard Vanderwell. *Designing Worship Together: Models and Strategies for Worship Planning.* Herndon, VA: Alban Institute, 2005.

Doran, Carol and Thomas H. Troeger. *Trouble at the Table: Gathering the Tribes for Worship.* Nashville: Abingdon, 1992.

Dozer, Dan. *Come Let Us Adore Him: Dealing with the Struggle over Style of Worship in Christian Churches and Churches of Christ.* Joplin, MO: College Press, 1994.

DuBois, W. E. B. *The Souls of Black Folk.* 1903. New York: Dover, 1994.

Duck, Ruth C. *Finding Words for Worship: A Guide for Leaders.* Louisville: Westminster John Knox, 1995.

Dudley, Grenae D. and Carlyle F. Stewart III. *Sanfoka: Celebrations for the African American Church.* Cleveland: United Church, 1997.

Dyrness, William A. *Senses of the Soul: Art and the Visual in Christian Worship.* Eugene, OR: Cascade Books, 2008.

Dyson, Michael Eric. *Between God and Gangsta Rap: Bearing Witness to Black Culture.* New York: Oxford Univ. Press, 1996.

Easum, William. *Dancing with Dinosaurs: Ministry in a Hostile and Hurting World.* Nashville: Abingdon, 1993.

Ellinwood, Leonard. *The History of American Church Music.* New York: Morehouse-Gorham, 1953.

Erskine, Noel Leo. *From Garvey to Marley: Rastafari Theology.* Gainesville: Univ. Press of Florida, 2005.

Esken, Harry and Hugh T. McElrath. *Sing with Understanding: An Introduction to Christian Hymnody.* 2nd ed. Nashville: Church Street, 1995.

Evans, Jr., James H. *We Have Been Believers: An African-American Systematic Theology.* Minneapolis: Fortress, 1992.

———. *We Shall All Be Changed: Social Problems and Theological Renewal.* Minneapolis: Fortress, 1997.

Fisher, Miles Mark. *Negro Slave Songs in the United States.* New York: Citadel, 1953.

Floyd, Jr., Samuel A. *The Power of Black Music: Interpreting Its History from Africa to the United States.* New York: Oxford Univ. Press, 1995.

Frame, John M. *Worship in Spirit and Truth: A Refreshing Study of the Principles and Practice of Biblical Worship.* Phillipsburg, NJ: P & R Publishing, 1996.

Franklin, Robert M. *Another Day's Journey: Black Churches Confronting the American Crisis.* Minneapolis: Fortress, 1997.

Gaddy, C. Welton. *The Gift of Worship*. Nashville: Broadman, 1992.

Gay, Kathleen. *African-American Holidays, Festivals, and Celebrations: The History, Customs, and Symbols Associated with Both Traditional and Contemporary Religious and Secular Events Observed by Americans of African Descent*. Detroit: Omnigraphics, 2007.

Getui, Mary N. *Theological Methods and Aspects of Worship in African Christianity*. Nairobi, Kenya: Acton, 1998.

Goatley, David Emmanuel. *Were You There? Godforsakenness in Slave Religion*. Maryknoll, NY: Orbis Books, 1996.

Gonzalez, Justo L. *¡Alabadle! Hispanic Christian Worship*. Nashville: Abingdon, 1996

Hackett, Charles D. and Don Saliers. *The Lord Be with You: A Visual Handbook for Presiding in Christian Worship*. Cleveland: OSL, 1990.

Hansen, Marsha. *My Soul Is a Witness: The Message of the Spirituals in Word and Song*. Minneapolis: Augsburg Books, 2006.

Harris, Michael W. *The Rise of Gospel Blues: The Music of Thomas Andrew Dorsey in the Urban Church*. New York: Oxford Univ. Press, 1992.

Hawn, C. Michael. *Gather Into One: Praying and Singing Globally*. Grand Rapids: William B. Eerdmans, 2003.

———. *One Bread, One Body: Exploring Cultural Diversity in Worship*. Herndon, VA: Alban Institute, 2003.

Hickman, Hoyt L., Don E. Saliers, Laurence Hull Stokey, and James White. *The New Handbook of the Christian Year*. Nashville: Abingdon, 1992.

Hinson, Glenn. *Fire in My Bones: Transcendence and the Holy Spirit in African American Gospel*. Philadelphia: Univ. of Pennsylvania, 2000.

Hoffman, Lawrence A. and Janet R. Walton, eds. *Sacred Sound and Social Change: Liturgical Music in Jewish and Christian Experience.* Notre Dame: Univ. of Notre Dame Press, 1992.

Holck, Jr., Manfred, compiler. *Dedication Services for Every Occasion.* Valley Forge: Judson, 1984.

Hollies, Linda H. *A Trumpet for Zion: Year A.* Cleveland: Pilgrim, 2001.

———. *A Trumpet for Zion: Year B.* Cleveland: Pilgrim, 2002.

———. *A Trumpet for Zion: Year C.* Cleveland: Pilgrim, 2003.

Holmes, Jr., Zan W. *Encountering Jesus.* Nashville: Abingdon, 1992.

Hood, Robert E. *Begrimed and Black: Christian Traditions on Blacks and Blackness.* Minneapolis: Fortress, 1994.

———. *Must God Remain Greek? Afro Cultures and God-talk.* Minneapolis: Fortress, 1990.

Hoon, Paul Waitman. *The Integrity of Worship.* Nashville: Abingdon, 1971.

Hooper, William L. *Ministry and Musicians: The Role of Ministry in the Work of Church Musicians.* Nashville: Broadman, 1986.

Hopkins, Dwight N. *Heart and Head: Black Theology—Past, Present, and Future.* New York: Palgrave, 2002.

———. *Introducing Black Theology of Liberation.* Maryknoll, NY: Orbis Books, 1999.

———. *Shoes That Fit Our Feet: Sources for Constructive Black Theology.* Maryknoll, NY: Orbis Books, 1993.

Hunter, James Davison. *Culture Wars: The Struggle to Define America.* New York: Basic Books, 1991.

Hurston, Zora Neale. *The Sanctified Church.* Berkeley, CA: Turtle Island, 1981.

Hustad, Donald P. *Jubilate II: Church Music in Worship and Renewal.* Carol Stream, IL: Hope, 1993.

————. *Jubilate! Church Music in the Evangelical Tradition.* Carol Stream, IL: Hope, 1981.

Jackson, Irene V., ed. *Afro-American Religious Music: A Bibliography and Catalogue of Gospel Music.* Westport, CT: Greenwood, 1979.

Johansson, Calvin M. *Discipling Music Ministry: Twenty-first Century Directions.* Peabody, MA: Hendrickson, 1992.

————. *Music and Ministry: A Biblical Counterpoint.* 2nd ed. Peabody, MA: Hendrickson, 1998.

Johnson, Miccolo Jason. *Soul Sanctuary: Images of the African American Worship Experience.* New York & Boston: Bulfinch, 2005.

Jones, Arthur C. *Wade in the Water: The Wisdom on the Spirituals.* Maryknoll, NY: Orbis Books, 1993.

Jones, Cheslyn, Geoffrey Wainwright, Edward Yarnold, and Paul Bradshaw, eds. *The Study of Liturgy*, rev. ed. Oxford: Oxford Univ. Press, 1992.

Jones, Joseph. *Why We Do What We Do: Christian Worship in the African-American Tradition.* Nashville: R. H. Boyd, 2006.

Jordan, James. *Evoking Sound: Fundamentals of Choral Conducting and Rehearsing.* Chicago: GIA, 1996.

————. *The Musician's Soul.* Chicago: GIA, 1999.

————. *The Musician's Spirit: Connecting to Others through Story.* Chicago: GIA, 2002.

————. *The Musician's Walk: An Ethical Labyrinth.* Chicago: GIA, 2006.

Keener, Craig S. and Glenn Usry. *Defending Black Faith: Answers to Tough Questions about African-American Christianity.* Downers Grove, IL: InterVarsity, 1997.

Keikert, Patrick R. *Welcoming the Stranger: A Public Theology of Worship and Evangelism.* Minneapolis: Fortress, 1992.

Kirk-Duggan, Cheryl A. *African American Special Days: 15 Complete Worship Services.* Nashville: Abingdon, 1996.

———. *Exorcizing Evil: A Womanist Perspective on the Spirituals.* Maryknoll, NY: Orbis Books, 1997.

———. *More African American Special Days: 15 Complete Worship Services.* Nashville: Abingdon, 2005.

———. *Soul Pearls: Worship Resources for the Black Church.* Nashville: Abingdon, 2003.

Kroeker, Charlotte, ed. *Music in Christian Worship.* Collegeville, MN: Liturgical Press, 2005.

Labberton, Mark. *The Dangerous Act of Worship: Living God's Call to Justice.* Downers Grove, IL: InterVarsity, 2007.

Lewis, Tamara E. *Plenty Good Room: A Bible Study Based on African American Spirituals.* Nashville: Abingdon, 2002.

Liesch, Barry. *The New Worship: Straight Talk on Music and the Church.* Grand Rapids: Baker Book, 1996.

Lincoln, C. Eric and Lawrence Mamiya. *The Black Church in the African American Experience.* Durham: Duke Univ. Press, 1990.

The Liturgy Documents: A Parish Resource. 3rd ed. Chicago: Liturgy Training, 1991.

Long, Thomas G. *Beyond the Worship Wars: Building Vital and Faithful Worship.* Herndon, VA: Alban Institute, 2001.

Lovelace, Austin C. and William C. Rice. *Music and Worship in the Church.* Nashville: Abingdon, 1976.

Lovell, Jr., John. *Black Song: The Forge and the Flame.* New York: Macmillan, 1972.

Mapson, Jr., J. Wendell. *The Ministry of Music in the Black Music.* Valley Forge: Judson, 1984.

———. *Strange Fire: A Study of Worship and Liturgy in the African American Church.* St. Louis: Hodale, 1996.

Marshall, Madeleine Forell. *Common Hymnsense.* Chicago: GIA, 1995.

Maynard-Reid, Pedrito U. *Diverse Worship: African American, Caribbean, & Hispanic Perspectives*. Downers Grove, IL: InterVarsity, 2000.

McClain, William B. *Come Sunday: The Liturgy of Zion*. Nashville: Abingdon, 1990.

McGann, Mary E. *Let It Shine: The Emergence of African American Catholic Worship*. New York: Fordham Univ. Press, 2008.

———. *A Precious Fountain: Music in the Worship of an African American Catholic Community*. Collegeville, MN: Liturgical Press, 2004.

Measels, Donald Clark, ed. *Music Ministry: A Guidebook*. Macon, GA: Smyth & Helwys, 2004.

Migliore, Daniel L. *Faith Seeking Understanding: An Introduction to Christian Theology*. Grand Rapids: William B. Eerdmans, 1991.

Miller, Barbara Day. *The New Pastor's Guide to Leading Worship*. Nashville: Abingdon, 2006.

Mitchell, Robert H. *I Don't Like That Music*. Carol Stream, IL: Hope, 1993.

Mitchen, Stephanie. *Name IT and Claim IT: Prosperity Preaching in the Black Church*. Cleveland: Pilgrim, 2007.

Muchimba, Felix. *Liberating the African Soul: Comparing African and Western Christian Music and Worship Styles*. Colorado Springs: Authentic, 2007.

Myers, Kenneth A. *All God's Children and Blue Suede Shoes: Christians and Popular Culture*. Wheaton, IL: Crossway Books, 1989.

Nelson, Timothy J. *Every Time I Feel the Spirit: Religious Experience and Ritual in an African American Church*. New York: New York Univ. Press, 2005.

Nichols, Stephen J. *Getting the Blues: What Blues Music Teaches Us about Suffering and Salvation*. Grand Rapids: Brazos, 2008.

Niebuhr, H. Richard. *Christ and Culture*. New York: Harper & Row, 1951.

Noland, Rory. *The Heart of the Artist: A Character-Building Guide for You and Your Ministry Team*. Grand Rapids: Zondervan, 1999.

Orr, N. Lee. *The Church Music Handbook for Pastors and Musicians*. Nashville: Abingdon, 1991.

Owens, Bill. *The Magnetic Music Ministry*. Nashville: Abingdon, 1996.

Pass, David B. *Music and the Church: A Theology of Church Music*. Nashville: Broadman, 1989.

Peretti, Burton W. *Lift Every Voice: The History of African American Music*. Lanham, MD: Rowman & Littlefield, 2009.

Pinn, Anthony B. *The Black Church in the Post-Civil Rights Era*. Maryknoll, NY: Orbis Books, 2002.

Pitts, Jr., Walter F. *Old Ship of Zion: The Afro-Baptist Ritual in the African Diaspora*. New York: Oxford Univ. Press, 1993.

Plantinga, Cornelius Jr. and Sue A. Rozeboom. *Discerning the Spirits: A Guide to Thinking about Christian Worship Today*. Grand Rapids: William B. Eerdmans, 2003.

The Psalms: An Inclusive Language Version Based on the Grail Translation from the Hebrew. Chicago: GIA, 2000.

Raboteau, Albert J. *A Fire in the Bones: Reflections on African-American Religious History*. Boston: Beacon, 1995.

———. *Slave Religion: The "Invisible Institution" in the Antebellum South*. New York: Oxford Univ. Press, 1978.

Ramshaw, Gail. *Christian Worship: 100,000 Sundays of Symbols and Rituals*. Minneapolis: Fortress, 2009.

Reagon, Bernice Johnson, ed. *We'll Understand It Better By and By: Pioneering African American Gospel Composers*. Washington, DC: Smithsonian Institution, 1992.

Redman, Robb. *The Great Worship Awakening: Singing a New Song in the Post-Modern.* San Francisco: Jossey-Bass, 2002.

Reed, Teresa L. *The Holy Profane: Religion in Black Popular Music.* Lexington: Univ. Press of Kentucky, 2003.

Reid, Stephen Breck. *Listening In: A Multicultural Reading of the Psalms.* Nashville: Abingdon, 1997.

———. *Psalms and Practice: Worship, Virtue, and Authority.* Collegeville, MN: Liturgical Press, 2001.

The Revised Common Lectionary: The Consultation on Common Texts. Nashville: Abingdon, 1992.

Routley, Erik. *Church Music and the Christian Faith.* Carol Stream, IL: Agape, 1978.

———. *Twentieth Century Church Music.* Carol Stream, IL: Agape, 1964.

Saliers, Don E. *Worship as Theology: Foretaste of Glory Divine.* Nashville: Abingdon, 1994.

———. *Worship Come to Its Senses.* Nashville: Abingdon, 1996.

Sample, Tex. *Powerful Persuasion: Multimedia Witness in Christian Worship.* Nashville: Abingdon, 2005.

Sanders, Cheryl J. *Saints in Exile: The Holiness-Pentecostal Experience in African American Religion and Culture.* New York: Oxford Univ. Press, 1996.

Satterlee, Craig A. *When God Speaks through Worship: Stories Congregations Live By.* Herndon, VA: Alban Institute, 2009.

Scheer, Greg. *The Art of Worship: A Musician's Guide to Leading Modern Worship.* Grand Rapids: Baker Books, 2006.

Schilling, S. Paul. *The Faith We Sing: How the Message of Hymns Can Enhance Christian Belief.* Philadelphia: Westminster, 1983.

Schultze, Quentin J., et al. *Dancing in the Dark: Youth, Popular Culture, and the Electronic Media.* Grand Rapids: William B. Eerdmans, 1991.

Segler, Franklin M. *Understanding, Preparing for, and Practicing Christian Worship.* 2nd ed. rev. Randall Bradley. Nashville: Broadman & Holman, 1996.

Senn, Frank. *Christian Liturgy: Catholic and Evangelical.* Minneapolis: Fortress, 1997.

Simpson, Eugene Thamon. *Hall Johnson: His Life, His Spirit, and His Music.* Lanham, MD: Scarecrow, 2008.

Smith, Efrem and Phil Jackson. *The Hip-Hop Church: Connecting with the Movement Shaping Our Culture.* Downers Grove, IL: InterVarsity, 2005.

Smith, Kathleen S. *Stilling the Storm: Worship and Congregational Leadership in Difficult Times.* Herndon, VA: Alban Institute, 2006.

Smith, William S. *Joyful Noise: A Guide to Music in the Church for Pastors and Musicians.* Franklin, TN: Providence House, 2007.

Smith-Pollard, Deborah. *When the Church Becomes Your Party.* Detroit: Wayne State Univ. Press, 2008.

Southern, Eileen. *Readings in Black American Music.* New York: W. W. Norton, 1971.

———. *The Music of Black Americans: A History.* 3rd ed. New York: W. W. Norton, 1997.

Spencer, Donald A. *Hymn and Scripture Selection Guide: A Cross-Reference Tool for Worship Leaders.* Grand Rapids: Baker Book House, 1993.

Spencer, Jon Michael. *Black Hymnody: A Hymnological History of the African-American Church.* Knoxville: Univ. of Tennessee Press, 1992.

———. *Protest and Praise: Sacred Music of Black Religion.* Minneapolis: Fortress, 1990.

———. *Sing a New Song: Liberating Black Hymnody.* Minneapolis: Fortress, 1995.

Stewart III, Carlyle F. *African American Church Growth: 12 Principles for Prophetic Ministry*. Nashville: Abingdon, 1994.

———. *Black Spirituality and Black Consciousness: Soul Force, Culture and Freedom in the African-American Experience*. Trenton, NJ: Africa World, 1999.

———. *Soul Survivors: An African American Spirituality*. Louisville: Westminster John Knox, 1997.

Talbot, Frederick H. *African American Worship: New Eyes for Seeing*. Lima, OH: Fairway, 1998.

Thompson, Bard. *A Bibliography of Christian Worship*. Metuchen, NJ: American Theological Association & Scarecrow, 1989.

Tozer, A. W. *Tozer on Worship and Entertainment*. James L. Snyder, comp. Camp Hill, PA: Christian Publications, 1997.

Uzukwu, E. Elochukwu. *Worship as Body Language: Introduction to Christian Worship: An African Orientation*. Collegeville, MN: Liturgical Press, 1997.

Van Dyk, Leanne. *A More Profound Alleluia: Theology and Worship in Harmony*. Grand Rapids: William B. Eerdmans, 2004.

Vanderwell, Howard, ed. *The Church of All Ages: Generations Worshiping Together*. Herndon, VA: Alban Institute, 2008.

Vann, Jane Rogers. *Gathered before God: Worship-Centered Church Renewal*. Louisville: Westminster John Knox, 2004.

Vitz, Paul C. *Psychology as Religion: The Cult of Self-Worship*. 2nd ed. Grand Rapids: William B. Eerdmans, 1994.

Wahl, Thomas Peter. *The Lord's Song in a Foreign Land*. Collegeville, MN: Liturgical Press, 1998.

Walker, Wyatt Tee. *Somebody's Calling My Name: Black Sacred Music and Social Change*. Valley Forge: Judson, 1979.

———. *Spirits that Dwell in Deep Woods: The Prayer and Praise Hymns of the Black Religious Experience*. 1987, 1988, 1991. Edited by James Abbington. Chicago: GIA, 2003.

Wallace, Robin Knowles. *Things They Never Tell You before You Say "Yes": The Nonmusical Tasks of the Church Musician.* Nashville: Abingdon, 1994.

Warren, Gwendolin Sims. *Ev'ry Time I Feel the Spirit: 101 Best-Loved Psalms, Gospel Hymns, and Spiritual Songs of the African-American Church.* New York: Henry Holt, 1997.

Washington, James Melvin. *Conversation with God: Two Centuries of Prayers by African Americans.* New York: HarperCollins, 1994.

Watkins, Ralph C. *The Gospel Remix: Reaching the Hip Hop Generation.* Valley Forge: Judson, 2007.

Webber, Robert E. *Ancient-Future Time: Forming Spirituality through the Christian Year.* Grand Rapids: Baker Books, 2004.

———. *Planning Blended Worship: The Creative Mixture of Old and New.* Nashville: Abingdon, 1998.

———. *Rediscovering the Christian Feasts: Services of the Christian Year.* Peabody, MA: Hendrickson, 1998.

———. *Rediscovering the Missing Jewel: Worship through the Culture.* Peabody, MA: Hendrickson, 1997.

———. *Renew Your Worship: A Study in the Blending of Traditional and Contemporary Worship.* Peabody, MA: Hendrickson, 1997.

———. *Worship Is a Verb: Eight Principles for Transforming Worship.* 2nd ed. Peabody, MA: Hendrickson, 1995.

Westermeyer, Paul. *The Church Musician.* rev. ed. Minneapolis: Augsburg Fortress, 1997.

———. *Let Justice Sing: Hymnody and Justice.* Collegeville, MN: Liturgical Press, 1998.

———. *Te Deum: The Church and Music.* Minneapolis: Fortress, 1998.

———. *With Tongues of Fire: Profiles in 20th-Century Hymn Writing.* St. Louis: Concordia, 1995.

Williams, Juan and Quinton Dixie. *This Far by Faith: Stories from the African American Religious Experience.* New York: HarperCollins, 2003.

Wilmore, Gayraud S. *Last Things First: Library of Living Faith.* Philadelphia: Westminster, 1982.

Wilson-Bridges, Flora. *Resurrection Song: African-American Spirituality.* Maryknoll, NY: Orbis Books, 2001.

Wilson-Dickson, Andrew. *The Story of Christian Music.* Minneapolis: Fortress Press, 1996.

Wimberly, Anne E. Streaty. *Nurturing Faith & Hope: Black Worship as a Model for Christian Education.* Cleveland: Pilgrim, 2004.

———. *Soul Stories: African American Christian Education.* Nashville: Abingdon, 1994.

Wimbush, Vincent L., ed. *African Americans and the Bible: Sacred Texts and Social Textures.* New York: Continuum International, 2000.

Witvliet, John D. *The Biblical Psalms in Christian Worship: A Brief Introduction and Guide to Resources.* Grand Rapids: William B. Eerdmans, 2007.

———. *Worship Seeking Understanding: Windows into Christian Practice.* Grand Rapids: Baker Academic, 2003.

Woods, Robert and Brian Walrath. *The Message in the Music: Studying Contemporary Praise & Worship.* Nashville: Abingdon, 2007.

Wren, Brian. *Praying Twice: The Music and Words of Congregational Song.* Louisville: Westminster John Knox, 2000.

Wright, Jr., Jeremiah A. *Africans Who Shaped the Faith: A Study of 10 Biblical Personalities.* Chicago: Urban Ministries, 1995.

Wuthnow, Robert. *Christianity in the 21st Century: Reflections on the Challenges Ahead.* New York: Oxford Univ. Press, 1993.

———. *Re-discovering the Sacred: Perspectives on Religion in Contemporary Society.* Grand Rapids: William B. Eerdmans, 1992.

Discography

The following pages contain information regarding sound recordings of Black sacred music that are available through GIA Publications, Inc. The list is organized in reverse chronological order and provides the following data: Year of Release, Title, Catalog Number, Description and Contents. A recording of relevance to the essays in this volume, but not available through GIA, is the companion compact disc for *Beams of Heaven: Hymns of Charles Albert Tindley (1851–1933)*. See the end of Chapter 5 for more information.

Year of Release: 2008
Title: 42 Treasured Favorites from the *African American Heritage Hymnal*
Cat. No.: CD-742

Description:
With this recording GIA hopes to preserve the tried-and-true treasures of the African American religious experience.

Recorded at Omega Recording Studios, Rockville, MD and St. Luke Church in McLean, VA.

Contents:
Disc 1
1. Bless the Lord
2. Welcome into This Place
3. Father, I Stretch My Hands to Thee
4. Guide My Feet
5. God Is
6. Be Still My Soul
7. God Will Take Care of You
8. How Great Thou Art

9. To God Be the Glory
10. Great Is Thy Faithfulness
11. The Lord Is My Light
12. Old Time Religion
13. Yes, God Is Real
14. Siyahamba
15. Come, Thou Font of Every Blessing
16. O For a Thousand Tongues to Sing
17. He Will Remember Me
18. Jesus, Keep Me Near the Cross
19. Lead Me to Calvary
20. At the Cross

Disc 2

1. All Hail the Power of Jesus' Name
2. Let It Breathe on Me
3. Softly and Tenderly Jesus Is Calling
4. Come Out of the Wilderness
5. Leaning on the Everlasting Arms
6. It Is Well with My Soul
7. Just a Little Talk with Jesus
8. The Solid Rock
9. Walking Up the King's Highway
10. We've Come This Far by Faith
11. We'll Understand It Better By and By
12. Where Could I Go?
13. Keep Me, Every Day
14. This Day
15. Thy Way, O Lord
16. Lead Me, Guide Me
17. Satan, We're Gonna Tear Your Kingdom Down
18. Something Within
19. We Shall Walk through the Valley in Peace
20. Blessed Assurance, Jesus Is Mine
21. This Little Light of Mine
22. We're Marching to Zion

Year of Release: 2008

Title: Use Me: 17 Selections from the African American Church Music Series

Cat. No.: CD-741

Description:

The fifth recording of titles from GIA's African American Church Music Series.

Recorded at Omega Recording Studios, Rockville, MD.

Contents:

1. Use Me
2. Done Made My Vow
3. There Is a Fountain
4. Deep River
5. He's Been Keeping Me
6. He Stooped to Bless
7. Come We That Love the Lord
8. He Sleeps
9. I Know I Got Religion
10. Rejoice in the Lord Always
11. Precious Lord
12. In the Word
13. Ride Up in the Chariot
14. Late One Night Mary Had a Baby
15. Savior, Lead Me
16. Lord, I Don' Don'
17. Dwell in the House

Year of Release: 2007
Title: 46 More Hidden Treasures from the *African American Heritage Hymnal*
Cat. No.: CD-711

Description:

A second volume of lesser-known titles from the *African American Heritage Hymnal*.

Recorded at Omega Recording Studios, Rockville, MD and St. Luke Church in McLean, VA.

Contents:
Disc 1

1. In the Beauty of Holiness
2. We've Come to Worship You
3. Be Still, God Will Fight Your Battles
4. Cast Your Cares
5. Oh, What He's Done for Me
6. God Never Fails
7. Oh, the Glory of Your Presence
8. The Lamb
9. While We Are Waiting, Come
10. Rise Up, Shepherd, and Follow
11. Behold the Star
12. Jesus, Remember Me
13. I See a Crimson Stream
14. Because He Lives
15. All Hail the Power of Jesus' Name
16. Glorious Is the Name of Jesus
17. So Glad I'm Here
18. Holy, Holy, Holy! Lord God Almighty
19. Unity
20. Welcome to My Father's House
21. New Born Again
22. The Lily of the Valley
23. I Can Do All Things through Christ

Disc 2

1. Acceptable to You
2. I Love the Lord, He Heard My Cry
3. In Christ There Is No East or West
4. What a Friend We Have in Jesus
5. Bless This House
6. Until I Found the Lord
7. Even Me
8. The Lord Is Blessing Me Right Now
9. He Has Done Great Things for Me
10. He's Sweet, I Know
11. Precious Memories
12. Bridegroom and Bride
13. The Gift of Love
14. It's Alright
15. I Thank You, Jesus
16. Thank You, Jesus
17. Lord, Make Me More Holy
18. Till We Gather Again
19. Be with Us All, Lord
20. The Lord's Prayer
21. Wash, O God, Our Sons and Daughters
22. Lord, I Have Seen Thy Salvation
23. Jesus Is Here Right Now

Year of Release: 2006
Title: Beams of Heaven: 18 Selections from the African American Church Music Series
Cat. No.: CD-653

Description:
The fourth recording of titles from GIA's African American Church Music Series.

Recorded at Omega Recording Studios, Rockville, MD.

Contents:

1. Beams of Heaven
2. Bless the Lord
3. Fix Me, Jesus
4. He Is God
5. I Must Tell Jesus
6. I Will Look to the Hills
7. Lord, Rebuke Thy Servant Not
8. O Hide Me
9. I Will Make the Darkness Light (Hymn Version)
10. I Will Make the Darkness Light (Solo Version)
11. I Will Make the Darkness Light (Gospel Version)
12. Where Shall I Go
13. Psalm 150
14. Shout for Joy
15. We Are Our Heavenly Father's Children
16. He Sweet, I Know
17. The Lord Will Make a Way Somehow
18. Oh, Glory!

Year of Release: 2005
Title: 49 Hidden Treasures from the *African American Heritage Hymnal*
Cat. No.: CD-636

Description:
The first of two volumes of lesser-known titles from the *African American Heritage Hymnal*.

　　Recorded at Omega Recording Studios, Rockville, MD and St. Luke Church in McLean, VA.

Contents:
Disc 1

1. Lord, Keep Me Day by Day
2. When in Our Music God Is Glorified
3. Day and Night Praise

4. Hallelujah, Amen
5. Amen Siakudumisa
6. The Angels Keep a-Watchin'
7. God Is a Wonder to My Soul
8. Guide Me, O Thou Great Jehovah
9. Halleluya! We Sing Your Praises
10. Hail to the Lord's Anointed
11. Where Shall I Be?
12. A Stable Light Lamp Is Lighted
13. Messiah Now Has Come
14. Heaven's Christmas Tree
15. Brightest and Best
16. A Perfect Sacrifice
17. Just for Me
18. Lift High the Cross
19. O Sacred Head, Sore Wounded
20. Oh, the Blood of Jesus
21. I Know It Was the Blood
22. Touch Me, Lord Jesus
23. I Know That My Redeemer Lives
24. The Strife Is O'er

Disc 2

1. Spirit of Go, Descend upon My Heart
2. Spirit Song
3. Deeper, Deeper
4. Renew Thy Church, Her Ministries Restore
5. Just As I Am
6. We Offer Christ
7. He Knows Just What I Need
8. All My Help Comes from the Lord
9. The Decision
10. We Won't Leave Here Like We Came
11. O Holy Savior
12. There's a Bright Side Somewhere
13. O Thou, in Whose Presence

14. The Storm Is Passing Over
15. Remember Me
16. In Me
17. Here Am I
18. He's Done So Much for Me
19. Shine on Me
20. Thuma Mina
21. Koinonia
22. My Soul Loves Jesus
23. The Crown
24. Mayenziwe
25. If You Live Right

Year of Release: 2005
Title: How Excellent Is Thy Name: 15 Selections from the African American Church Music Series
Cat. No.: CD-630

Description:
The third recording of titles from GIA's African American Church Music Series.
Recorded at Omega Recording Studios, Rockville, MD.

Contents:
1. How Excellent Is Thy Name
2. Striving after God
3. O Magnify the Lord
4. Le's Have a Union
5. Song of Thanksgiving
6. Wait on the Lord
7. Hold On
8. Try Jesus
9. Travelin' Shoes
10. My Eternal King
11. Something Within
12. My Peace I Leave with You

13. May the Work I've Done Speak for Me
14. Bound for Canaan's Land
15. It Pays to Serve Jesus

Year of Release: 2004
Title: Spirits That Dwell in Deep Woods: The Prayer and Praise
    Hymns of the Black Religious Experience
Cat. No.: CD-605

Description:
Wyatt Tee Walker's original volumes of prayer and praise hymns from 1885 to 1925 have been collected and recorded. This CD features not only the hymns, but the singing style of the period as well.

Recorded at the Chicago Center for the Performing Arts, Chicago, IL.

Contents:
1. Another Day's Journey and I'm So Glad
2. Blessed Be the Name of the Lord
3. Daniel in the Lion's Den
4. Glory, Glory! Hallelujah
5. Great Change Since I've Been Born
6. I Know His Blood Has Made Me Whole
7. I Know I Got Religion, Yes, Yes!
8. I Know My Name Is Written There
9. I Wanna Be Ready
10. I Wanna Die Easy
11. I'm Glad I Got That Old Time Religion
12. Jesus Is a Rock in a Weary Land
13. Jesus on the Mainline
14. Keep Your Lamps Trimmed and Burning
15. Lord, Have Mercy
16. Nobody But You, Lord
17. Satan, We're Gonna Tear Your Kingdom Down
18. Something Happened When He Saved Me
19. Something on the Inside Working on the Outside
20. Talkin' 'bout a Good Time

21. Till I Die, Till I Die
22. You Better Min'
23. You Better Run
24. You Can't Make Me Doubt Him

Year of Release: 2003
**Title: Guide My Feet: 14 Selections from the African American
    Church Music Series**
Cat. No.: CD-600

Description:
The second recording of titles from GIA's African American Church Music
Series.
    Recorded at Clinton Studios, New York, NY.

Contents:
1. Guide My Feet
2. The Lord's Prayer
3. Sing to the Lord
4. Seek the Lord
5. Psalm 1
6. We Are Climbing Jacob's Ladder
7. It Is Well with My Soul
8. Go Where I Send Thee
9. My Soul Is Anchored in the Lord
10. Great Is Thy Faithfulness
11. Worthy Is the Lamb
12. The Precious Blood of Jesus
13. Jesus, You Brought Me All the Way
14. Someday

Year of Release: 2003
**Title: Catholic Classics, Volume 7: African American Sacred
    Songs**
Cat. No.: CD-557

Description:
Volume 7 in GIA's Catholic Classics CD Series.
    Recorded at Bias Recording Company, Inc., Springfield, VA.

Contents:
  1. Soon and Very Soon
  2. Taste and See
  3. Lead Me, Guide Me
  4. He Touched Me
  5. Were You There
  6. Mary's Canticle
  7. In the Garden
  8. It Is Well with My Soul
  9. Precious Lord, Take My Hand
  10. There Is a Balm in Gilead
  11. Softly and Tenderly Jesus Is Calling
  12. We've Come This Far by Faith

Year of Release: 2002
**Title: Stop By, Lord: 14 Selections from the African American
    Church Music Series**
Cat. No.: CD-540

Description:
The first recording of titles from GIA's African American Church Music
Series, which includes anthems, spirituals, and gospel selections.
    Recorded at Clinton Studios, New York, NY.

Contents:
  1. Stop By, Lord
  2. Sing to the Lord
  3. Nobody Knows the Trouble I See

4. O for Faith
5. Good News, the Savior Is Born!
6. Stand by Me
7. Lord, Make Me an Instrument
8. Rock-a My Soul
9. More Love to Thee
10. The Lord Will Hear the Just (*with* Proclaim God's Marvelous Deeds)
11. It's My Desire
12. Speak to My Heart
13. Taste and See
14. Sanctify Me

Year of Release: 1999
Title: Mass of St. Cyprian
Catalog No.: CD-462

Description:
A live recording of *The Mass of Saint Cyprian* by composer Kenneth W. Louis.

Recorded at Holy Comforter-Saint Cyprian Catholic Church, Washington, DC.

Contents:
1. The Procession
2. Lord, Have Mercy
3. Glory to God
4. Responsorial Psalm: Proclaim God's Marvelous Deeds
5. Gospel Acclamation: Alleluia
6. Offertory: I'm Willing, Lord
7. Preface Acclamation: Holy, Holy
8. Memorial Acclamation: Dying You Destroyed Our Death
9. Great Amen
10. Our Father
11. Lamb of God
12. Communion Hymn: Taste and See
13. Jesus, You Brought Me All the Way

Year of Release: 1995
Title: I Call Upon You God!
Catalog No.: CD-342

Description:
Featuring the *Mass of Saint Martin de Porres* by Leon Roberts.
Recorded at Lion & Fox Recording, Washington, DC.

Contents:
1. I Call upon You, God!
2. Lord, Have Mercy
3. Glory to God in the Highest
4. Taste and See the Goodness of the Lord
5. Alleluia
6. General Intercessions
7. I Surrender All
8. Holy, Holy, Holy
9. Keep in Mind
10. Great Amen
11. The Lord's Prayer/Doxology
12. Lamb of God
13. Jesus Is Here Right Now!
14. Mary's Canticle
15. His Eye Is on the Sparrow
16. Give Us Peace

Year of Release: 1994
Title: Take Me to the Water: Thirteen New Spiritual
Arrangements
Catalog No.: CD-329
by Alice Parker

Description:
Featuring Pamela Warrick-Smith, contralto, and musicians of Melodious Accord.
Recorded at Chapel of the Riverside Church, New York, NY.

Contents:

1. I Know the Lord
2. Stayed on Jesus
3. Come On Up to Bright Glory
4. Don't Be Weary, Traveler
5. Hush! Hush!
6. We Will March thru the Valley
7. He Is King of Kings
8. Let Us Break Bread Together
9. Is There Anybody Here
10. Free at Last
11. Take Me to the Water
12. Cert'nly, Lord
13. Who'll Be a Witness

Year of Release: 1981
Title: He Has the Power: The Mass of St. Augustine
Catalog No.: CD-160
by Leon Roberts

Description:

Featuring *The Mass of St. Augustine* by Leon Roberts.
  Recorded at Omega Sound Studios, Kensington, MD.

Contents:

1. Thank You, Lord
2. Lord, Have Mercy/Gloria
3. Responsorial Psalm
4. Alleluia
5. Holy, Holy, Holy!
6. Christ Has Died
7. Doxology/The Lord's Prayer/Lamb of God
8. Remember Me/He Has the Power